Journey from Innocence to Experience

Writings of F Scott Fitzgerald

Journey from Innocence to Experience

Writings of F Scott Fitzgerald

Manasi Sinha

Decent Books
New Delhi

ISBN 81-86921-02-8

First Published in India : 1998

Published by
Decent Books
'Suryodaya'
D-36-A/1, Mohan Garden
Najafgarh Road
New Delhi - 110 059

Distributed by
D.K. Printworld (P) Ltd.
'Sri Kunj', F-52, Bali Nagar
New Delhi - 110 015
Phones: (011) 545-3975; 546-6019 Fax: (011) 545-5926

Printed by
DP's Impressive Impressions, New Delhi - 110 059

Preface

THE present study intends to examine the fiction of F. Scott Fitzgerald as a whole. But the autobiographical aspect of Fitzgerald's fiction and its representative quality as related to the Jazz Age — two aspects on which there has been so much insistence — have not been ignored.

In the twenties, following the great success of his first novel, Fitzgerald had appealed to the public more for the charm of his personality and his role of spokesman for a generation than for his artistic achievement. Praised as the creator of a disenchanted, but at the same time, sentimental attitude towards experience, he was overwhelmingly present in the public's mind and in the gossip columns. In the thirties, the fallacious reasons for which he had been admired in the previous decade offered the pretext for an almost general condemnation. What had at first appeared as representative of an age was overturned by the failure and collapse of that age, and for a good span of time the writer appeared as a lonely survivor for a period that had wrecked American society with its irresponsible attitude. Relegated into the background by a wave of puritanical prudery, Fitzgerald died a bitter and early death without completing the novel that was to redeem him in the eyes of the public.

The life, too of Fitzgerald was a sharply divided life in every sense. The years of his youth, of his first maturity and his early success in the 1910s and 1920s contrast markedly with the years full of personal and public happenings that led to his premature death in 1940. But Fitzgerald's life was divided above all in a personal and human sense. It was divided between the pursuit of the artistic ideal and the continual, too frequent concessions to the taste of the moment or to the lure of easy success. He was a victim, in so many ways, of the myth of success and money.

Fitzgerald's history, in fact, is the history of a journey — a journey from innocence to experience which has to be interpreted in the light of the alternations of these two terms and the oscillations between them. Innocence is the pristine integrity of the naive, wild-eyed childlike selfhood. And experience is the abandonment of innocence through entry into the adult, sexual, moneyed life. Fitzgerald's novels are a record of the strenuous journey — to and fro — from dreaming youth to maturity. In the words of Fitzgerald, " . . . innocence is no end in itself and as our minds unwillingly matured we began to see New York whole. . . ."[1]

In the Introduction — 'The Man and the Artist', we have taken note of the fact that Fitzgerald's life and work are so interwoven that the distinction between them blurs. In a sense, Fitzegerald imagined and created his life and lived in his fictional protagonists. It appears from a study of Fitzgerald's life and works that he believed that the author must live as his characters live. In living up to a dream, an ideal of dramatic selfhood, Fitzgerald merged both his personality and the society in which he lived into his artistic representation.

The American Dream is the subject of the first chapter. This dream, it has been pointed out, is so deep-rooted in American life, that its presence can be felt in almost every sphere of it, attributing certain typical characteristics to the nation. The overwhleming presence of this dream has enriched American literature and has made it unique (Chapter 1).

Manifestation of the American Dream is evident as early as in Thomas Jefferson's *The Declaration of Independence*. And great

1. F. Scott Fitzgerald, "My Lost City", *The Crack-Up*, p. 29.

writers, like Emerson, Thoreau, and Whitman, were prophets of this dream. They believed in the perfectibility of man and hoped for a new society of free and self-reliant individuals. They enthusiastically affirmed that the dream was both good and realisable. But there were traditionalists too, like Hawthorne and Melville, who believed in the innate depravity of man. They thought the effects of the dream to be disastrous – yielding to delusions only. They denounced the falsity of the dream (Chapter 2).

But the American Dream, though it starts withering, persists in a new shape and this persistence of the American dream is the subject-matter of the next chapter. In the two following chapters it has been pointed out that American literature has evolved under the influence of the everchanging American life. American literary scene has sensitively responded to each and every change in the social and cultural milieu of American life. Transcendental vision of the great writers of 'the golden day' could not satisfy the pragmatic realists. This realistic group was concerned with the depiction of reality as they saw it – mostly the materialistic and ugly reality of the existing society. But it has been pointed out, these new ideas reflected merely a change of mood. While criticizing the dream as vague and impossible, some of the writers in the later ages still cherished the ideals latent in it. The indirect treatment and even the negative implications of the dream also signified the influence of the dream in the writings of the new era (Chapters 3 and 4).

The dream persisted, at least for a little while, because World War I, which made Europe impoverished and paralysed, made the world of 1920 richer and more comfortable to the millions of Americans. The total atmosphere was full of gaiety and recklessness. It was F. S. Fitzgerald, one of the central figures of the period, who named the era – the Jazz Age. The post-War decade in America was significant for the rise of the youth. Everyone now seemed to belong to the younger generation and the younger generation seemed to be everywhere. The new code of morals along with the new freedom were alluring and illusive. The "new generation dedicated more than the last to the fear of poverty and the worship of success" were being haunted by their dream of 'success' and 'money'. "In these days", in the words of Fitzgerald, "life was like the race in *Alice in Wonderland*, there was a prize for everyone." [2] But it was not so easy to break with the traditional values of life overnight and the new code, which was born in disillusionment persisted to be a disillusioning one for a decade and could not substitute the richness and the strength of the old-ordered life. So the American Adam lay disenchanted and innocence gave way to experience (Chapter 5).

A typical American youth of the period is Amory Blaine (in Fitzgerald's first novel (*This Side of Paradise*). He is, at the beginning, fresh, vital and innocent with 'penetrating green eyes' and a 'facile imaginative mind'. During his stay at Minneapolis "the crude and vulgar air of Western civilisation first catches him". (p.18) After he came to Princeton, his puritan conscience made him see the cities "as one vast juvenile intrigue". (p. 59) He could not save himself from being entrapped into this intrigue. Amory's early skirmishes with girls and events that follow make him 'experienced' and breaks his illusion that youth is innocent, permanent and indestructible. Taken as a whole, Fitzgerald's fiction testifies to his talent for identifying the corruption and moral failure marked by the surface glitter and carnival antics of the 1920s. But Amory's experience ultimately made him wise to realise the difference between the world of dreams and the world of reality and prompted him "to help in building up the living consciousness of the race" (p.265). He belonged to the generation, yet his faith in life kept him above, since through loss and isolation he had learnt to know himself; he had "escaped from a small enclosure into a great labyrinth. He was where Goethe was when he began Faust" (p.264) (Chapter 6).

---

2. "Echoes of the Jazz Age", *The Crack-Up*, p. 21.

This gap between the world of dreams – of expectations and the world of reality and the decay of the romantic dream is also indicated in the life of Anthony Patch in Fitzgerald's second novel *The Beautiful and the Damned*. Anthony's inability to adjust his romantic self with the materialistic society makes him suffer and ultimately be ruined. He is duped by his own desire. The seeds of his destruction lay within his dream. Through Anthony's decay Fitzgerald reveals another important feature of his time – the reckless life of the youth without any regard for the past. *The Beautiful and the Damned* is a parable on the deceptiveness of dreams, and on the impossibility of evading reality through illusion. Fitzgerald was faithful to his own vision of the world and he tried his best to express the same in his own characteristic way (Chapter 7).

Fitzgerald's third novel *The Great Gatsby* took him a step forward towards attaining maturity in thought as well as style and made his depiction of the withering of the American dream more vivid and life-like. This novel is a saga of an innocent abroad – an idealistic dreamer who reposes his trust on the unlimited possibilities of life without being aware of the tragic destiny that awaits him. His chequered career suggests the shortcomings of the American's idealized conception of himself in relation to the external world. Gatsby fails to recognise his complicity in the corrupt world ruled by Mammon of which he had become a part. And he also fails to understand the real Daisy Fay Buchanan – the American nightingale with money in her voice who has long ago 'lost her white girlhood in the moral debacle which followed the Great War'. In this he represents the naive American youth still capable of envisioning the dream of the first Dutch explorers as they viewed the 'fresh, green breast' of Long Island three centuries before. Gatsby incarnates the pulls of dream and illusion, the recurrent cycles of youth's capacity for wonder by which the New World has been dominated since the very beginning. The objective rendering of the intensely personal experience of Gatsby indicates Fitzgerald's seriousness of purpose and his maturity of vision. As a result Gatsby transcends reality and time, he belongs not exclusively to one epoch of American civilization but to history inasmuch as all history repeats in cycle form what Gatsby represents – America itself and the hollowness of the American dream.

But the point is not so much that the dream has been corrupted, the main fact is that it always carried within it the seeds of its own corruption. Fitzgerald called his next novel *Tender is the Night*, 'My Testament of Faith'. And it is really a testament of his faith and the title is significant. The nine years between *The Great Gatsby* and *Tender is the Night* were years of frustation and despair for Fitzgerald. Hence Fitzgerald's decision to write 'a novel of our time' inevitably meant to show the break-up of a fine personality and to use insanity as the appropriate image of modern life. Gatsby had survived the onslaught of reality spiritually intact; Fitzgerald determined now to show a man who is a natural idealist and who in his attempt to rise to the top of the social world loses his idealism and talent and his dream. Dick Diver was a dreamer who had set his illusions up against the power of reality and so ultimately was doomed to failure. Diver's discovery that he simply lacks the strength and will to impose his sense of order on the flux of existence, is nothing but Fitzgerald's admission as a creative artist of his own failure to exert his will on the brutal dictatorship of American reality. Dick Diver sacrifices his work to Nicole and his will to the seductive lure of the tender night; he retracts from the hard glare of reality into the 'Verdous Gloom' where forgetfulness anaestizes time and drugs the will. The defeat of Dick Diver, his surrender to Mammon, marks not merely the abandonment of an idealized though constructive approach to life, but also confirms the anarchic nature of human existence (Chapter 9).

That materialistic and anarchic powers would inevitably dominate, is also Fitzgerald's thesis in *The Last Tycoon*. Fitzgerald in this last unfinished novel records and examines the death of a set of value – of traditional individualism defeated in part by its own contradiction and in part by a plutocracy which has lost or never known the humanistic value once associated with individualism. *The Last Tycoon* is the story of Monroe Stahr – a once-powerful and dominating personality, who, struggling with changing social patterns, and with personal confusions and inner conflicts, falls into moral and spiritual bankruptcy. Monroe Stahr is actually the echo of an earlier age, the last of a line; Stahr is powerless to resurrect the vigour of such an age. The past cannot be retrieved, neither can it resuscitate itself – its fate, lke Stahr's, is to die (Chapter 10).

From *This Side of Paradise* to *The Last Tycoon* is a long journey. Fitzgerald in his earlier novels, while indicating the oscillation between innocence and experience has focused upon the gradual decline of moral and spiritual values. But in *The Last Tycoon*, his focus shifted, or widened, to include the elements of rebirth and historical repetition. Although the actual past was irretrievable, the pattern of the past might nevertheless be expected to repeat in the future. As far as Fitzgerald's work was concerned, then, *The Last Tycoon* did represent a new way of looking at certain phenomena – specially 'a modified way of looking at the decline of the West'.

The unlimited possibilities of mankind, its strength and resistance against the opposing fate may provide a constant inducement to sing; but there is little doubt that the repeated failure of dream are constantly brought into the foreground. Fitzgerald records failures and frustrations while projecting continually on that background a reaffirmation of the purity of the dream of his characters. In an ordinary and everyday dimension he repeats the parable embodying the aspiration and the lament of a whole nation. In his fiction can be found the glory and the pathos of the American experience at large.

Contents

Introduction
The Man and the Artist

CREATIVITY is too elusive, too fundamentally mysterious to afford a point by point correspondence between the man and his art and hence the relation between the artist's personality and his work, though obviously intimate can never be made wholly explicit.

F. Scott Fitzgerald's life and work are so interwoven that the distinction between them blurs. In a sense, Fitzgerald imagined and created his life and lived in the fictional protegonists. The quiet life of the conscientious writer was utterly foreign in Fitzgerald's conception of the writer's role. Rather it appears from a study of Fitzgerald's life and works that he believed that the author must live as his characters live, must make their style his own and his theirs. In living up to a dream, an ideal of dramatic selfhood, Fitzgerald merged both his personality and the society in which he lived into his artistic representations. It would be as true to say that his life was a novel in progress – and, like his last novel, unfinished – as that his novels are autobiographical. His characters starts as very different persons, confronted different moral issues but were transformed imperceptively, as he worked over them, into an image of the author himself. "Sometimes I don't know whether Zelda and I are real or whether we are characters in one of my novels",[1] Fitzgerald remarked in 1933. His sensibility constantly responsive to the world about him, cumulatively impelled him towards a 'brooding' on the image of America and the moral issues involved. But although his characters were frequently confronted with morel issues, the author was more interested in chronicling the delights and the decadence of the twenties than in coming to grip with the moral problems they raised.

By the early thirties, however, a series of personal misfortunes brought moral issues to the centre of his thought and made it necessary for him to develop ways of dealing with them. His misfortunes have been frequently related: his wife was mentally ill and was at length confined permanently to a sanitarium. He himself was plagued with alcoholism – the party was over but the hangover seemed permanent. He was disppointed with his writing. None of it had brought him the financial rewards he had anticipated and he was constantly in debt. He seemed in the thirties to be suffering the consequences of a misspent youth, and he experienced a growing sense of guilt and a need to pass some sort of moral judgement upon himself and the decade that had come to such an abrupt climax in 1929.

In the writing he did during the last ten years of his life, three elements connected with this need constantly recur. First there is the idea of failure and non-fulfilment that appears conspicuously in most of his short stories, and also in *Tender is the Night,* and in *The Crack-Up.* Second, there is the concern with the morality of wealth, most evident in *Tender is the Night.* Finally, and most important, there is the problem of individual moral responsibility. Though this last is the landscape for nearly all of Fitzgerald's later works, it is most succinctly revealed in the climax he had outlined for *The Last Tycoon.*

In at least four of Fitzgerald's later short stories his feelings of both guilt and failure become abundantly clear. Each of the four – *Three Hours Between Planes, The Long Way Out, The Lost Decade,* and *Babylon Revisited* – is a hyperbolic treatment of the author's sense of non-fulfilment and remorse about the immediate circumstances of his own life.

Three Hours Between Planes is the story of Donald Plant, who pays a visit to a childhood sweetheart, exchanges confidences and kisses with her, and then discovers she has mistaken him for someone else. The success he had felt at recapturing the past and moulding it to the image he had desired – the girl had cared little for him when they were both young – dissolves. Plant has failed, but not through any fault of his own. "The second half of life is a long process of getting rid of things",[2] says Fitzgerald through Donald Plant, and the attempt to relive an earlier age in terms of later knowledge is impossible.

The author himself was attempting to get rid of a number of things and was having little success in doing so. Faced with the personal consequences of the twenties, he seemed unable to throw them off. He was still an alcoholic, still dissatisfied with his writing, still in debt. Most important, in terms of this story, he still had within him the image of his wife Zelda as she had been in the first years he knew her. He felt he had to extirpate this image and accept the fact that she would not recover from her illness.

The Long Way Out has a similar emphasis upon the idea of failure or lack of fulfilment, and again the protagonist is not directly responsible for the outcome. Mrs. King, a victim of schizophrenia, is sufficiently improved to be granted a few days' leave from the sanitarium to be with her husband. Mr. King, however, is killed in an automobile accident and never arrives to meet her. When she is told of his death, she has a serious relapse, refuses to believe the news, and each day thereafter waits patiently and mindlessly for him to arrive.

The parallel with Zelda is obvious. Arthur Mizener, commenting upon Fitzgerald's attitude towards his wife's illness, remarks:

> Despite the doctors' assurances that Zelda's trouble went back a long way, and that nothing he could have done would have prevented it, Fitzgerald had a deep feeling of guilt about it. He knew how much he was to blame for the irregularity of their lives; he knew what he had contributed to that 'complete and never renewed break

of confidence' which had occurred in Paris in 1929. . . .[3]

In these two stories the element of guilt is suggested not by the failure of the characters concerned, but rather by the author's choice of subject-matter.This is somewhat true also of *The Lost Decade*. Here, however, the hyperbole becomes more extravagant. Louis Trimble, an architect, is shown around New York by the point-of-view character who has the impression that Trimble has been away from the city for ten years. The latter learns finally that the architect has simply been drunk for a decade. The sense of failure is overwhelming. The reader does not learn why this has happened to Trimble; he learns only that a promising and talented man has wasted years of his life. Again the personal parallel is clear. Mizener suggests that Trimble is intended as a personification of lost generation of the twenties. It is more likely that Trimble represents the colossal dissipation that Fitzgerald had come to believe himself guilty of.

Babylon Revisited is probably the best of these four stories, and it deals not only with personal frustration and failure, but with the problems of money, liquor, and moral responsibility as well. Charlie Wales, a reformed pleasure-seeker, returns to Paris, hoping that his sister-in-law Marian will give him the custody of Honoria, his little daughter. Marian cannot forget, however, that Charlie had, in a drunken stupor, contributed to his wife's death by locking her out in the snow. When some carousing friends of Charlie's appear on the scene and begin to reminisce about the good old days, her mind is made up, and she refuses to permit him to take his daughter away with him.

Fitzgerald frankly admitted the personal nature of this story. In a letter to his daughter he told her that she was a character in *Babylon Revisited*. What he felt had been the irresponsible treatment of his wife he expressed in terms of a situation that had led to her death. His inability to fulfil what he thought were the responsibilities of fatherhood he described in terms of a parent who was all believed to be a menace to the welfare of his child. Charlie like Scott Fitzgerald in his own life makes no searching examination and offers no convincing explanation of the reasons of his previous misdeeds. It was very well to attribute the 'lunacies' of the twenties to the war, or to too much money, or to immaturity but these were not reasons but rationalizations, unable to go any further than this. The author could not give such dimension to the character of Charlie Wales.

A fatalistic determinism likewise marks the only novel Fitzgerald completed after 1939 – *Tender is the Night*. If the short stories just discussed represent a hyperbolic treatment of some of the circumstances of Fitzgerald's own life, the novel traces the moral decline and fall of practically everyone. The men and women that inhabit the novel are no longer the daring, fun-loving throng of the author's earliest vision of the twenties. They are unsavoury couples with dissolving marriages, Americans dying in barroom brawls. The moral themes of the novel are the same as those in the short stories, and the resolution of moral issues is handled the same way.

The central figure of *Tender is the Night* is Dick Diver, a psychiatrist who, one can't help noticing, is singularly unable to diagnose his own psychic ills. The book charts Diver's course downward from professional promise and personal happiness to utter obscurity and moral decay. The reader's last glimpses of Diver find him moving to smaller and smaller towns in upstate New York; rumour has it that his last move was occasioned by an unpleasant affair he had with one of his patients.

The problem as it is faced by Dick Diver is essentially a moral one. It is Nicole, first Diver's patient and then his wife, who brings about his confrontation with great wealth and who is the agent of his decline. Her fortune is ever swelling, and as the news of its increase is brought, throughout the novel, by one character or another, one comes to feel that money is the dynamic, inexorable force that drives Diver downward. Not only does he lack the strength to give his life a purpose in the face of such wealth, but he is also unable to free himself from its enervating effects after Nicole has left him.

The fate of Dick Diver furnishes another insight into Fitzgerald's later moralism and the nature of his contrition for past sins. To him it was believable that a man should lose his zest for work, his desire to make any contribution to society, if the profit motive is removed. And without work a man's character crumbles. This begins to sound remarkably like the Protestant ethic. If profit is, then, to some extent the measure of virtue, the fact that Fitzgerald's writing didn't sell served to aggravate the frustrations of his other personal adversities. It increased his sense of guilt without increasing his understanding. Dick Diver is perhaps the most appealing personality Fitzgerald ever created, and one cannot regard his face with indifference. The answer, of course, lies partly in the nature of the time Diver is living in. His self-knowledge was attained before the war and hence it is no longer adequate in the face of new needs. He has been destroyed by forces he could neither control nor even fully understand, and the moral judgement he had once possessed was of no use.

Fitzgerald's own world was crumbling and he was willing to admit that a large measure of responsibility was his. But apparently admission was not enough, for he continued to be plagued with increasing evidence of sin. It was the conflict between his own sense of justice and that which seemed to be imposed upon him from outside that helped produce *The Crack-Up*. In attempting to lighten the oppressive weight of what seemed to be evil of his own creation, he employed both cynicism and an almost unconscious blame of others.

The fragment of a novel that Fitzgerald left at his death is in some ways anticlimactic. It seems almost as though the author has effectively passed judgement upon his life and work in *The Crack-Up*, and might have been spared the effort of a literary second coming. A causal glance at *The Last Tycoon* seems to indicate that he had, indeed, broken sharply with his earlier writing and had chosen a new and very different subject.

Yet the difference is more apparent than real. It is obviously the work of the same man, no longer preoccupied with the sparkle and then the tarnish of the twenties, but still grappling with the same kinds of problems. The setting is Hollywood; the tycoon of the title is Monroe Stahr, a young and highly talented motion picture director. It is in Stahr that the reader sees the residue Fitzgerald thought he himself had been left with after the close of the post-war decade. Though he is only in his thirties, Stahr is destined for an early death. The tycoon's doctor shakes his head dolefully after each examination and sees in his patient an urge toward total exhaustion, "a perversion of the life force. . . ."[4]

This is not intended to be a novel of new beginnings or of a new point of view. Though social and economic matters intrude themselves more frequently in *The Last Tycoon* than in other of Fitzgerald's novels (problems of labour unions and depression wages, for example) the personal and moral issues remain uppermost. Perhaps it could not have been otherwise. The difficulties that the author had first faced in the twenties were not yet solved and he was ever aware of the weight of the past. In *The Last Tycoon* this legacy is symbolized by the fact that Monroe Stahr falls in love with a woman to whom he was first attracted because she resembled his dead wife. Neither he nor Fitzgerald had broken with the past.

When read in terms of image and symbol, *The Last Tycoon* is the personal statement of a writer who was fumbling for a way to reorganize the ingredients of his shattered life into an artistic whole. The world had moved on but the novelist had not His last sizeable work was permeated with a feeling of decline and decay. that hung over all its characters. He continued to be torn by an ambivalence that thrust him back and forth between the two poles of innocence and experience.

References

1. *The Stories of F. S. Fitzgerald* (with an Introduction by Malcolm Cowley), New York: Scribner's 1951, p. XII.

2. "Three Hours Between Planes", *Ibid.*, p. 469.

3. Arthur Mizener, *The Far Side of Paradise*, Boston: Houghton Mifflin Company, 1965, p. 241.

4. F. S. Fitzgerald, *The Last Tycoon*, New York: Scribner's 1970, p. 108.

1

American Dream

THE ambivelence that thrust Fitzgerald back and forth between the two poles of innocence and experience owned its existence to the American dream to the ultimate withering of that dream.

American Dream is older than America itself. The millennial hope for paradise and perfection contained in the dream is as old as human mind. In a sense, the constant yearning and search for 'a brave new world' – the very essence of the dream led, in fact, to the discovery of America. Prior to that discovery even, America had its existence as a state of mind or a dream. From the very beginning of the Western civilization people had dreamt of a better and newer way of life in some new country full of peace and prosperity. This hope for a new life full of premises is eternal and universal. Only with the changes in time it has a different shape and got a different name such as 'Millennium', 'Revelation', 'Golden Age', 'Utopia', etc. All these are various names of the same objective, that is an ideal condition of life. The locale of earthly paradise always shifted with the change in the cult of faith prevalent at different times. But essentially the dream was always placed in some land of imagination. 'Eden' or 'Heaven', 'Atlantis' or 'Utopia' whatever might have been the name, the place was far away from realities and beyond the reach of man. Only the discovery of the island "that flowered once for Dutch Sailors' eyes – a fresh green breast of the new world"[1] made possible the localisation of the dream and the land of imagination become a geographical reality. A few years after the fisrt voyage of Columbus, Thomas More's *Utopia* in 1515 held out the promise of this bright fresh world across the sea. Ever since then America has been associated with the myth of paradise and perfection, progress and prosperity. But the dream, though all along present at the root of American life, got its specific name only in 1931, in writings of J.T. Adams. In his *Epic of America* he described "... that dream of a better, richer and happier life for all our citizens of every rank which is the greatest contribution we have as yet made to the thought and welfare of the world".[2]

Captain Edward Johnson, who came to Massachusetts with the first wave of settlers in 1630, in his *Sion's Saviour* announced the new continent to be the chosen place where the Lord will create a new Heaven, and a new Earth. So he asked the "Oppressed, Imprisoned and Scurrilously derived" to gather together for being "Shipped for His Service, in the Western World", to escape for once and all the errors of a corrupt and weary old world "for planting the united colonies of New England". Indeed, to the Calvinist settlers of New England, America seemed to be the Land of Canaan, to which God directed them as He once directed the children of Israel.

The accounts of Renaissance explorers encounraged the revitalisation of the old myth and suggested thier actual realisation on the American soil. Plato's *Philosophic Republic* or Thomas More's *Utpoia* seemed no more to be unattainable. The new-found-land appeared to be the land of 'Pearls and Plenty' where simple primitive people lived happily 'after the manner of the golden age'. According to some critics the islands on Atlantics "swept by the balmy breezes inhabited by natives of peaceful dispositions, living without toil or industry on the natural production of a generouis soil"[3] appeared as the ideal Commonwealth in Shakespeare's drama also.

Gonzalo, in *The Tempest* perceived the ideal Commonwealth as a place where –

> All things in common nature should produce
> Without sweat or endeavour: treason, felony,
> Sword, pike, knife, gun, or need of any engine,
> Would I do not have: but nature should bring forth,
> Of its own kind, all foison, all abundance,
> To feed my innocent people.[4]

Michael Drayton, Shakespeare's contemporary, spoke of the new colony as "Earth's only Paradise". Again John Donne thought of it as a land where future generations might witness 'the growth thereof to perfection'. Even almost a century after the first settlement Bishop Berkley spoke of America as that "happy clime . . . the seat of innocence where nature guides and virtue rules".[5] (*In Landmarks of American Writing,* edited by Hennig Cohen, 1970, p. 35). The 'Soft Primitivism' of Shakespeare can be found in Cervantes too. His description of Island of Bartaria under the rule of Good Sancho reminds one of the type of ideal society which was commonly believed to be existing in the new world (America). America offered the true image of an ideal society in a new and uncontaminated environment as man should have made in the beginning.

Like the soft primitivists, the admirers of harder primitivism found new possibilities in America. The native sons in all their freshness as well as ruggedness, seemed to the good Fathers, as "replicas of Greek and Roman exemplars of stoic and republican virtues".[6] Perhaps, Hobbes was the only exception and from the travellers' accounts he derived his most unsympathetic view of a natural but brutal state of mankind.

In general, America was the image of the chosen land untouched by the evils of Western civilization. Its inhabitants in all "their nakedness, their disconcerning absence of shame, their simplicity"[7] seemed to have been untainted by original sin.

America embodied a new Eden where Adam could have his second chance and "this 'infant world still quite naked and at the breast' suddenly presented to a senescent world another chance, perhaps the last one, to build anew the city of man."[8] In fact, the new world attracted the adventurers more and more and sheltered the displaced persons irrespective of their origin, colour and religion. It saved the distressed souls from slavery, starvation and persecutions. Thus America became a melting pot where the different nationalities mixed together and gave rise to a new nation called the Americans. And the precedent which Thomas More created in 1515 by locating his ideal state of *Utopia* in the newly discovered land, continued to be followed in the next centuries. America,'the place', where the religious prophecies of Isaiah could be fulfilled, furnished an opportunity to construct an ideally rational society and test the same against actuality. Ever since then, again and again "the myth of a timeless perfection in Utopia or heaven has become projected the temporal future of America".[9]

From the very moment of birth of the continent, American dream has been one of the chief motivating forces of American history. The dream is so much deep-rooted in American life, that its presence can be felt almost in every sphere of it attributing certain typical characteristics to the nation. Therefore, the dream is regarded as a national dream and it is difficult to give an exact definition of such a dream. Following John Steinbeck we can call "the wide and general dream" as "the American Way of Life".[10]

The overwhelming presence of the dream has enriched American literature and has made it unique. "American Literature", says Carpenter, "has differed from English because of the constant and omnipresent influence of the American dream upon it."[11] But he thinks this influence to be indirect and unconscious since the dream has remined a dream because of its inherent suggestiveness of 'an unconsciousness contradiction or unreality'. The original ambivalence of the old millennial hope, though in a different form, persisted in American dream too. Yet the dream has been the distinction of American literature.[12]

The American dream which was like a rebirth, the eternal, haunting craving of man to start again from the very beginning, expressed that yearning for a new life. Essentially it embodied an idea of progress toward a better life based on liberty and equality. Perfection was to be achieved not in the 'Kingdom of God' but in this new world. Of course, the colonial America was mostly Puritan sticking to the old ways of orthodoxy. So the New England mind could indulge in dream only at some enthusiastic moments and that too with certain amount of disbelief and doubt. The dream was affirmed only after American Revolution when America emerged as an independent nation, free from the old chains of tradition.

This dream was also affirmed and the manifestation of this aspect of the American spirit came to be evident even in Thomas Jefferson's *The Declaration of Independence*. Great writers like Emerson, Thoreau, Whitman and many others who believed in the perfectibility of man and hoped for a new society of free and self-reliant individuals, became prophets of this dream.

References

1. F. S. Fitzgerald, *The Great Gatsby*, New York: Scribner's 1953, p. 182.
2. J. T. Adams, *The Epic of America*, Boston: 1931, p. VIII.
3. Robert E. Spiller, *et al.* (ed.); *Literary History of the United States*, New York: Macmillan, 1960. p. 192.
4. *The Tempest* in William George Clark and William Aldis Wright (ed.), *The Works of Shakespeare*, London: Macmillian, 1956, p. 8.
5. Robert E. Spiller, *et al.* (eds.), *Literary History of the United States*, New York: Macmillan, 1960, p. 193.
6. *Ibid.*, p. 192.
7. *Ibid.*, p. 194.
8. *Ibid.*, p. 192.

9. F. I. Carpenter, *American Literature and the Dream,* New York: Philosophical Library, Inc., 1955, p. 6.

10. John Steinbeck, "Paradox and Dream" in Douglas A. Hughes (ed.), *The Way It Is,* New York: 1970, p. 63.

11. F.I. Carpenter, *American Literature and the Dream,* New York: Philosophical Library, Inc., 1955, p. 3.

12. *Ibid.,* p. 6.

2

The Prophets of the Dream

In 1776, Thomas Jefferson, the philosopher statesman of the Republic, proclaimed the dream eloquently and made his famous declaration to the world – "We hold these truths to be self-evident, that all men are created equal, that they are endowed by their creator with certain inalienable rights; that among these are life, liberty and the pursuit of happiness."[1] The Declaration of Independence acted as the new testament and preached the gospel of liberty and equality. Its concept of popular sovereignty paved the path for the democratic ideal of progress. Its dream for pursuit of happiness inspired the literature of American Renaissance.

The burden of Declaration is present in St. Jean De Crevecoeur's *Letters of An American Farmer*. Crevecoeur, a foreigner to the soil, stayed in America for a long period and did much to encourage Franco-American relationship specially during the difficult time of post-war diplomacy. He was very close with Washington, Franklin and especially with Thomas Jefferson. His Rousseauistic attitude discovered an ideal society in America and he saw the American as 'a new man' acting on 'new principles'. In the 'perfect society' of America, he felt everyone to be "animated with the spirit of an industry which is unfettered and unrestrained, because each person works for himself . . . we have no princes for whom we toil, starve and bleed: we are the most perfet society now existing in the world. Here man is free as he ought to be. . . . "[2]

America seemed to him to be a land of unparalleled opportunity providing a 'great field of action', for the 'energy of future generations'. Crevecoeur's description of this ideal pastoralized society was influenced by French Romantic individualism and enlightenment. Life in reality was not so much idyllic as suggested by him. His emotional commitment to the American society made its *Letters* more than a mere reporting. He could perceive the artistic possibilities of native themes and materials and created literature out of it which marked the beginning of an American literary tradition. Under the mask of 'James the Farmer' he presented the major American theme of self-analysis and raised for the first time the great question, 'What is an American?' and 'What does it mean to be an American?' In order to answer the query he explored the gap between America as fact and America as ideal – the enduring problem of American life. He had his own feeling of trust and doubt, faith and disillusion while depiciting the hope underlying the myth of America as man's paradise and the tension arising from the constant struggle to realise it in actuality. He presented the dream in its eighteenth century form.

The American Revolution is considered as one of the most important steps in the progressive course of human improvement. It created an atmosphere where American dream could flourish on the concept of idealistic progress and perfection. There was an inherent love of liberty inherent to the soil, and that every love of individual liberty became the dream of transcendentalists in nineteenth century. The transcendentalists were 'the philosophers of dream' and they celebrated the dream of the free and self-reliant American. They felt that political independence alone was not sufficient to gain in self-reliance. They believed, 'Kingdom of God' exists in every individual self which can be realized on the earth. The real newness of the American life presented altogether a new world to them. Though they cherished their dream in the midst of romanticism yet they rejected the antique and future worlds of romanticism, and utopianism in favour of the world to-day. Their dream was to make the world more free and more democratic by making individual conscience free. So their cry was for 'intellectual independence'. In their dream for perfection they wished to transcend or go beyond the immediate realities. But it was not a Rousseauistic emotional escape; rather they tried to make use of real opportunities in life and real changes in the world brought about by science. The transcendental dreamers prepared the way for realism both in philosophy and fiction. Above all, it gave priority to free will, not a despotic one, but tempered through 'discipline of nature' and 'moral law'. Transcendental dream was a 'religious emotion' and like the dream in any other period it was 'a great act of faith' and great writers of the period like Emerson, Thoreau, Whitman, Hawthorne and Melville were the prophets of the dream.

Emerson, to start with, in whom one gets so close to the American spirit, was a product of democracy whose dream was to develop new ways of life in the new world. He felt that to realize the ideals of freedom and democracy as enunciated by *The Declaration of Independence*, it was necessary to do away with the genteel tradition. He revolted against the moral puritanism of the past and welcomed the modern scientific attitude but not a materialistic one.

Emerson looked to the 'auspicious signs of the coming days' and hoped for' the elevation of what was called the lowest class in the state' and the triumph of 'the near, the low, the common, instead of the sublime and beautiful'. He was interested in the "literature of the poor, the feelings of the child, the philosophy of the street, the meaning of household life", which he thought were the 'topics' of his time.[3] His philosophy of 'Self-Reliance' was for the attainment of the ideal, democratic self, the precondition for the achievement of true democracy. His trust in individual led him tc preach the message 'Trust Thyself' against the pessimism of 'modern temper' of his own time. He had his firm faith: "Nothing can bring you peace, but yourself. Nothing can bring you peace but the triumph of principles."[4] This strong faith in each and every individual 'self' reflects that love for liberty, freedom of spirit and a vision for glorious future. All his writings bear the mark of an ardent optimism and a great hope inherent in a dream since he believed in the possibility of realization of the democratic ideals of the dream.

Like Emerson, Thoreau too accepted the ideal of freedom and his deep concern was not only with the state of man but the promising condition of man. This eminent apostle of American Renaissance sought to make man free from economic and social traditions. He believed that, "There will never be a really free and enlightened state until the state comes to recognize the individual as a higher and independent power, from which all its own power and authority are derived, and treats him accordingly."[5] He protested against the cultural crudity and the materialism of the then America. He found his people to be 'pauperized and bleached' for lack of cultural enrichment and by being engrossed in the 'necessaries' of civil life they were getting afar from the civilization itself. He was a rebellious pioneer in search of an intellectual and moral frontier. His 'Civil Disobedience' sprang from this pioneer spirit of zest and adventure. He asked "for not at once no government, but *at once a* better government" and to have that better government it was the responsibility of an individual "to resist the seemingly irresistible".[6] But before doing so, he said, an individual must reform himself. His faith in personal revolution led him to reform himself before reforming society and virtually started an experiment with his own life in the primeval woods of Walden Pond. To him 'wilderness' provided a favourable locale to search for a more cultivated and civilized life and it served as the precondition of new morality and freedom. In the life of solitude, he looked to Nature as a gateway to higher state of culture for creating a better order of society. His stay at Walden was not a romantic escape to achieve perfection all at once; rather he tried with his idealism to start life anew in the swamps of Concord. In his own words —"I went to the woods because I wished to live deliberately, to front only the essential facts of life.

. . . I wanted to live deep and suck out all the marrow of life, to live so sturdily and Spartan-like as to put to rout all that was not life. . . . "[7] He aimed at self-discovery to escape the 'messianic delusion' and his dream of cultural enrichment and spiritual reawakening of the American, centred round the process of self-exploration. He aspired to achieve 'the flower and fruit of man', the 'ripeness'. Thoreau, 'the most clear-eyed of all American dreamers', as suggested by Carpenter, dreamed not of past times, but of reforming the American present; not of freedom in a world of fantasy, but in actuality; and not of immediate perfection, but of gradual improvement through individual effort. He accepted the dream cheerfully and believed that if one has built castles in the air one's work need not be lost, only one has to 'put foundations under them'. Thoreau the dreamer, felt that to meet with success it was necessary for an individual to advance confidently in the direction of his dreams and endeavour to live the life as he has imagined.

Along with Emerson and Thoreau, Whitman too affirmed the beauty of the dream and his mission was to 'strike up for a New World'. He celebrated the upsurge of the masses and the potentiality of the 'divine average'. He dreamed of popular democracy and his *Leaves* 'like a red flag', 'very brave and American' represent his hopes and dreams. Whitman, was, in fact, a dreamer and mystic in his inner life and his poetry is not the criticism of life, but a celebration of life. It is a song:

> Of Life immense in passion, pulse and power,
> Cheerful, for freest action form'd under the laws divine. . . . [8]

For him America is democracy and he desired to be the first spokesman for a new race of races in a democracy. His aim was to project the history of the future. In the manner of Emerson and Thoreau, he had a feeling of distrust towards the genteel tradition of the American past. He promised to 'report all heroism from an American point of view'. His ideal America was the country of revolt and in his reaction against European aristocratic culture he celebrated American 'barbarism'. This wild America to Whitman was the embodiment of freedom from European heritage and opportunities for the future to realize his democratic dream of the new world. The cause of the common man was a conquering religion to him and he named his Leaves as *Leaves of Grass* to indicate his appreciation for the qualities common to all. Grass, the common living thing in nature symbolized for him the victory of life.

> The smallest sprout shows there is really no death,
> And if ever, there was it led forwards life, and does not
> wait at the end to arrest it,
> And ceas'd the moment life appeared.[9]

While other writers of the age, Emerson for example – were busy with sublimating or intellectualizing the crude energy of American physical life, Whitman had a zest for 'magnificent bodies' and tried to establish a frank sensuality. He spoke of himself:

> I am the poet of the Body and I am the poet of the Soul.[10]

His song of 'Body Electric' gives expression to his idealistic opposition to the genteel orthodoxy. As body and soul are two aspects of the same verity, so also are evil and good and nothing in man was condemnable to him. He even included sin in his series of antitheses raised against the Puritanic morality and proclaimed himself to be 'the poet of sin' and 'the God of revolt-deathless sorrowful, vast'. In the defiant celebration of sin and evil his real purport was –

> Not to exclude or demarcate, or pick out evils from their formidable masses (even to expose them,)
>
> But add, fuse, complete, extend – and celebrate the immortal and the good.[11]

His ideal America was the country of revolt, but revolt to achieve the 'immortal good'.

Beneath the sensory experiences, spritual awareness was always there in him. He heard another song 'covering the earth and filling the spread of heaven', and felt an urge 'to ascend and enter the Unknown'. Whitman believed:

> But grander far the unseen soul of me, comprehending, endowing all those,
>
> Lighting the light, the sky and stars, delving the earth sailing the sea,
>
> (What were all those, indeed, without thee, unseen soul of, what amount without thee?)[12]

His 'passage to India' is a 'passage to more than India" and shadow of a greater dream. There he presented his synthesized view of 'the vision of the whole' achieving a sort of reconciliation of the past and present, man and nature, good and evil, 'the pleasures of heaven and the pain of hell'. His 'unpersuadable and relentless' 'brave soul' wished to 'sail forth – steer for deep water only'. 'Starting from fish-shape Paumanok' he 'journey'd with bold step and after roaming many lands' making an imaginary distant voyage to the land of 'primal thought', wished to reach –

> An unknown sphere more real I dream'd, more direct darts awakening rays about me, So long.[13]

Whitman through his dream of ideal democracy, a sort of spiritual democracy sought to achieve 'the moral elevation of huimanity' at large. His spirit responded to his country's spirit and he became 'the equalizer of his age and land'. 'Whatever satisfies the soul is truth' – this conviction of the poet shows how Whitman the dreamer is a seer too.[14]

References

1. Thomas Jefferson, "The Declaration of Independence", in Philip S. Foner, (ed.), *Basic Writings of Thomas Jefferson,* Willey Book

Company, 1944, p. 21.

2. John De Crevecoeur, *Letters From An American Farmer* (with an Introduction by Philips Bradley), Bombay: Popular Prakashan, 1964, p. 33.
3. R. W. Emerson, "The American Scholar", in William J. Fisher, *et al.* (eds.), *An Anthology of American Literature of the Nineteenth Century*, New Delhi: Eurasia Publishing House, 195, p. 68.
4. R. W. Emerson, "Self-Reliance", *Ibid.*, p. 82.
5. H. D. Thoreau, "Civil Disobedience", *Ibid.*, p. 134.
6. *Ibid.*, p. 116.
7. H. D. Thoreau, "Where I Lived and What I Lived For", *Ibid.*, p. 142.
8. Walt Whitman, "One's Self I Sing", *Leaves of Grass* (with an Introduction by S. K. Kumar), New Delhi: Eurasia Publishing House, 1962, p. 3.
9. "Song of Myself," *Ibid.*, p. 28.
10. *Ibid.*, p. 40.
11. "L. of G's Purport", *Ibid.*, p. 427.
12. "Grand Is The Seen", *Ibid.*, p. 428.
13. "So Long", *Ibid.*, p. 392.
14. "Preface 1855", *Ibid.*, p. XVII.

3

The Disenchanted

BUT the transcendental vision of the great writers of 'the Golden day' could not satisfy the pragmatic realists who emphasized the 'cash value' of the ideal. Resons for this change in vision are many and various.

American literature, in fact, has evolved under the influence of the ever-changing nature of American life. Literary life of the nation has sensitively responded to each and every change in the social and cultural, milieu of American life. The closing of the frontier brought an enormous change in the country. It marked the end of an era of expansion and unlimited opportunities. The days of pioneering with its restless energy, dominant individualism, love for freedom and philosophy of self-reliance were over. The Civil War put the nation into a phase of transition and turmoil of ideals. Free lands disappeared. Rapid industrialization introduced the days of interdependence and restricted liberty. Romanticism was replaced by cold philosophy of facts and scientific realism. The philosophers and writers of the day could not justify the high hopes of trans-cendental dreamers and criticised their abstraction of thoughts. They doubted the possibility of realising the dream of progress toward an absolute perfection. Deep faith in life was lost. "... American literature was launched upon an exciting exploration of non-traditional materials, form, and assumptions."[1]

Members of the optimistic group like Emerson, Thoreau and

Whitman believed in the perfectibility of man and hoped for a new society of free and self-reliant individuals. They enthusiastically affirmed that the dream was both good and realizable. In contrast, the traditionalists believed in the innate depravity of man. They thought that the individual with his 'wild original stain' was destined to be doomed in the struggle between good and evil in him and in the society, his own creation. Hawthorne and Melville shared this attitude of the traditionalists to a great extent. They criticized the transcendental dream of liberty on the ground that individual freedom as conceived by the 'Party of Hope' led to nothing but moral anarchy and ideal democracy was not possible. They thought the effects of dream to be disastrous yielding to delusion only. So they denounced the falsity of the dream. They were doubtful about the potentialities of the dream but were sympathetic to the ideals of it.

As regards Hawthorne, who abandoned the philosophic thought both of the past and of his New England contempraries, "clove his own path through the trackless realms of the moral life".[2] As a dreaming boy in Salem, he entered the moral labyrinth and was deeply concerned with the meaning of life. Amidst the turmoil of contemporary 'Philistine America' he took refuge in the secret solitude of his mind and presented the world immortal characters like Ethan Brand, Hester Prynne, Zenobia – 'the lonely children of his imagination'. His puritanic reflections upon these creations – men and women afflicted by a guilt or 'a stain upon the soil', wove an intricate web of inevitable involutions of moral pattern. His characters dreaming to set out for the new world got entangled in the web and all their ventures to go beyond the conventional code of morality led to utter disillusionment and made them denounce the falsity of dream.

Hawthorne's *Scarlet Letter* 'a tale of human frailty and sorrow', present the authentic American dream of freedom and independence. Through the character of Hester Prynne, Hawthorne projected both the greatness and the grim tragedy implicit in the dream. Hawthorne, in general, distrusted and discredited the dream of liberty and was doubtful whether individual freedom was truly desirable in this sinful world. But his own creation, Hester Prynne, envisioned the transcendental ideal of positive freedom and 'with her native energy of character, and rare capacity' she hoped for a new life in the wilderness of the new world. She was a dreamer of a new moral order and 'the world's law was no law for her mind".[3] Her universe was greater than 'the compass of the yonder town' where she lived and she knew it well that the forest track which led backward to the settlement led 'onward, too'. She repeatedly urged Dimmesdale to 'begin all anew' and exhorted him: "Exchange this false life of thine for a true one . . . Preach! Write! Act ! Do anything save to lie down and die."[4]

But Dimmesdale, no more the dreamer of the old Oxford days and, unlike Hester, a broken spirit, afraid to renounce the puritanic tradition merely fumbled: "O Hester . . . thou tellest of running a race to a man whose knees are tottering beneath him, I must die here! There is not the strength or courage left me to venture into the wide, strange, difficult world, alone!"[5] He simply bore the torment of the soul without any chance of resurrection of spirit, whereas Hester, in spite of her being branded an adulteress by the Puritan tribunal achieved a spiritual greatness through her dream; a dream not of romantic escape but of transcedental ideal of freedom. She did obey her heart and acted according to the dictates of her insitincts and thus remained true to her dream. The age Hester lived in " . . . . was an age in which the human intellect, newly emancipated had taken a more active and a wider range than for many centuries before. . . . Men . . . had overthrown and rearranged — not actually, but within the sphere of theory, which was their most real abode — the whole system wherewith was linked much of ancient principle. Hester Prynne imbided this spirit."[6]

Like Emerson and Thoreau, Hawthorne turned to intuition and not reason as the source of wisdom. Hester believed in a higher law. Her dream of liberty transformed her from an adulteress into the 'prophetess' of a new order of morality. Hawthorne with his deep moral instincts, of course, made her suffer for her love. He shared the belief of traditional authority that Hester sinned through her blind passion, and so, penalized her heavily and made her an outcast for the rest of her life. But according to the romantic view Hester's tragedy sprang from the evil of society. Further, according to the transcendental view, Hester sinned not by breaking the commandments, but violating the transcendental truth. She sinned by suppressing the identity of her husband to her lover and thereby deceiving the latter. She put romantic love ahead of ideal truth and in seeking to protect her lover by deception she sinned both against her own integrity and against God. Through her suffering Hawthorne depicted the grim tragedy implicit in the dream. Hester's dream of freedom clashed with the puritanic prejudices of her lover and she was doomed as a result of the tragic conflict between traditional morality and the transcedental dream. But in spite of the denigration and accusation resulting from the ostracisms of society and moral conviction of the author himself, Hester Prynne remains to serve as the embodiment of both the greatness as well as failure of American dream. Hawthorne's secret compassion for his creation made her ideal.

Unlike the other spokesmen of the period, Hawthorne could never feel that America was a new wold. " . . . . he felt the past weighing heavily on the present's back" and " . . . . he was more struck by decay than potentiality".[7] His next novel *The House of the Seven Cables* reveals this theme of frozen present and the negation of free will. Holgrave's remark"Shall we never have done with the corpse of the past?" brings out the cheerless spirit of the present. Hewthorne portrayed this young man in the image of Emerson's promising young American but not without the presentiment that the traditional values cast their asserting power over the coming generations and the posterity do partake the sin of the ancestors which make them sad and gloomy. So Holgrave even in his happy union with blooming Phoebe, which was a new life, could not avoid the delusion inherent in the dream.

Through Hawthorne could never feel that America was a new world and the new age was the dawn of unlimited possibilities, yet he closely examined its changing atmosphere, specially that of New England. *The Blithedale Romance* is a bolder revelation of Hawthorne's experience in the Utopian experiment of Brook Farm. The Blithedelian visionaries assembled together to start 'the life of Paradise anew'.[8] Their Quixotic enterprise embodied "the archetypal American experience: withdrawal from a corrupt society to form a regenerate community".[9] Hawthorne said in the preface that the novel was 'essentially a day-dream, and yet a fact' and he focused on the American dialectic between actual and ideal world. Blithedale, though not more than a day's walk from the old city, its promising environment made the visionaries feel "we had transported ourselves a world-wide distance from the system of society that shackled us at breakfast time".[10]

Hawthorne projected Blithedale experiment as the same old visionary hope of the early settlers in America. Miles Coverdale represented this Utopian optimism for a new life which, of course, ultimately turned into utter disillusionment. In his words " . . . . It was our purpose . . . (to show) mankind the example of a life governed by other than the false and cruel principles on which human society has all along been based." [11] it was his community's aim to 'profit by mutual aid' and to strive for 'love' for which they 'left the rusty iron frame-work of society' where "every son of woman both perpetrates and suffers his shares of the common evil, whether he chooses it or no".[12] Instead, the visionaries dreamed to establish the ideal community on the basis of human brotherhood. But this dream remained a day-dream, leading to delusion only, since Blithedale was found ultimately to be as false and hypocritical as the organized society of the established system.

The visionaries were perfect in their aim, but they lacked sincerity in their purposes. Person Ike Hollingsworth, "a cold, heartless, self-beginning and self-ending piece of mechanism", with his monomaniac egotism "subverts the nobler purpose of total regeneration embodied in the Blithedale community, destroying in the process also the faith and happiness of its other members".[13] His selfish principle was detected by Zenobia and she remarked, 'It is all self!' After spending 'the mad summer' with him she realized his moral obliquity and found in him: "Nothing else; nothing but self, self, self! . . . I see it now ! I am awake, disenchanted, disenthralled! Self, self, self!"[14] Zenobia's tragedy reflects the true fate of Blithedale which could not become a regenerate community as it dreamed to be. All visionary hopes and high ideals ended into delusion. The noble purpose of social perfection was vitiated and made impossible by ruthless individualism, the 'common evil' of the established system.

In *The Marble Faun* Hawthorne once again dealt in the same old theme of "ruthless influences of the past, the blight of wrong upon the completely innocent, the fellowship of sinners and the regenerative power of the sin".[15] *The Marble Faun* is the 'story of the fall of man'. In Donatello's loss of virtues Hawthorne posed the same problem of evil soiling utter innocence. This loss of innocence of course, initiated faun-like Donatello into the complexities of experience of the real world. His encounter with evil in the corrupt city transformed his primitive innocence into 'withering, sad, self-knowledge' and destroyed his Arcadian dream. Trained in Puritanic tradition Hawthorne believed in the regenerative value of sin. Miriam and Kenyon contemplated on this educative aspect of sin: "Was that very sin, – into which Adam precipitated himself and all his race, – was it the destined means by which, over a long pathway of toil and sorrow, we are to attain a higher, brighter and more profound happiness, than our lost birthright gave?"[16]

These characters convey Hawthorne's perplexity over sin as a necessary human condition. Hawthorne placed them against a 'dreadful blackness' where all their hopes and passions for happiness led them to despair and agony. They were "literally dreaming on the edge of precipice".[17]

While Hawthorne condemned the dream and stated in fictional terms the total impossibility of the dream, Melville believed in the ideals of the dream, but not in its victory. He affirmed the ideal of the dream but denied the fulfilment of it. In contrast with the members of the 'Party of Hope' like Emerson, Thoreau and Whitman he could not celebrate the democratic dream and its possible realization here and now. The stark realist in him made him aware of the dangers latent in the dream. But as regards the ideals, he always appreciated individual freedom and criticized the 'arbitrary laws' of the authority. His characters from Taji to Billy Budd – all possessed this virtue of natural freedom and were ennobled by the spirit of idealism. Even monomaniac Captain Ahab shared this instinctive democracy. But as far the real world was concerned Melville declared the impossibility of the ideal of liberty and accepted the authoritarian laws and the surrender of individual rights. His initial suggestion in 'Serenia' or 'White Jacket' that the ideal might be realized and his belief that 'Our Lord High Admiral will yet interpose' to set the right the world's wrongs gradually led him to declare that the arbitrary lines of conduct should be followed for the well-being of men.

And finally in *Billy Budd* he showed the execution of the ideally good man by the material law in the name of maintaining authoritarian discipline. Thus Melville hovered between the realm of ideals and the world of reality. His own dualism made his heroes suffer from a conflict to choose between the unattainable ideal and the unbearable real. This conflict between the democratic values and the autocratic cruelty created an absolute despair which finally turned into a mood of resignation or acquiescence. So we find Billy Budd voluntarily assenting to his own death-sentence acknoweldging the bitter truth that the defeat of goodness is inevitable. But Melville's originality lies in the fact that though he considered the American dream as something that 'shall not be' yet he proclaimed its desirablity. He was convinced that individual freedom though desirable was not possible in the world of actuality. Thus Melville was dreamer by conviction and not by faith; and he is regarded as the greatest critic of the American dream. While pointing out the dangers of the dream he held the most sympathetic view of it too.

Melville prophesized the failure of American dream and foretold the disasters to his age which expected the millennium. Unlike his countrymen who were concerned first with the utility of things, he sought to achieve the inner reality. He thought of the world in terms of Armageddon and of man as a 'fighting member of the world'. Melville first expressed his criticism of American dream in *Mardi*. Taji's imaginary travels around the imaginary archipelago of Mardi is, in fact, as Newton Arvin puts it, "the quest for an emotional security ... the quest for a just and happy sociality ... and the quest for an absolute and transcendent Truth."[18] This quest is much more than an adventure of the hero in *Typee*. *Mardi* reveals both his pride of being an American and his scepticism ragarding American's present and future.

Like his optimistic contemporaries Melville could not believe in the perfectibility of man for making democracy successful. Again, like Hawrthorne, he did not believe in the inevitable sinfulness of man. He accepted the ideals of freedom and equality but was aware of the limitation and helplessness of man arising out of conflict between good and evil. His lack of faith in human perfectibility led him to speak for the supremacy of authoritarian discipline and the prevalence of martial law.

Failure of democracy is a recurring theme in most of his works where Melville projected the life of the nation through the life of the crew either on a whaling ship or on a ship of war with captains as the 'leaders' whose order was final. Through his fiction Melville showed that democracy existed only in man's desire, not in the world of reality. Even where the setting is the whaling ship as in *Moby Dick*, where authoritarian principles were not absolute, democracy had very little chance to thrive. In short, the world to him was the same 'old battle-plain' and 'Mardi's peaces are but truces' making the dream a failure.

Moby Dick with its multifarious levels of meaning and interpretations depicts the tragedy of the democratic dream. Most critics view Captain Ahab, the democratic leader, to be the symbolic embodiment of the representative nineteenth century American, and the epic transmutation of American free enterpriser. "He is modern man, and particularly American man in his role as 'free' and 'independent' individual. . . . "[19] But Ahab, the democratic leader, was non-democratic in his action. He imposed his own will over the crew of his ship 'Pequod' in his fanatic pursuit of the 'Leviathan'. His 'excessive or neurotic self-dependence' led him to be a hero running against time and fighting against 'reality'.[20] He thought himself to be all-powerful as the omnipotent God and identified himself with all the mighty objects in the visible world.

This exessive self-pride is nothing but a distorted self-reliance which made him crazy and condemned the voyage of 'Pequod' into utter delusion. Ahab's indomitable will to dominate nature and his fanatic search for the white whale can be interpreted as a quest for the unattainable ideals in life. But his quest is not the quest of Ishmael, whose was " a quest for spiritual health, a desire to enter into a new and deeper harmony with creation".[21] Ishmael's attitude towards the white whale was of reverence and wonder and he accepted the mystery of creation and nature. But to Ahab it was symbol of evil. In his great hatred of it he waged a total war against it and for making his expedition a success he needed the willing help of the crew.

Ahab almost forced his fellowmen to follow an evil, even to the extent of the loss of their lives. He misled the crew and pursuaded them to seek after a false ideal of conquering evil with evil and thus caused self-destruction as well as the damnation of all. The crew represent the typical common people in democracy who are not in a position to choose between ideals and they became subservient to the intellectual domination of their Captain Ahab who is thought to represent the 'aristocracy of intellect'.[22] The tragic fate of the 'Pequod' is analogous to the fate of democracy. According to

Carpenter's analysis Melville suggested two possible factors responsible for the failure of democracy. 'The carelessness of the common people' and 'the confusion of its leaders' make the people give up their very democratic rights while pursuing the democratic ideal. So there is disillusionment resulting from the tragic confusion between good and evil and Melville wished to introduce order into moral universe.

To Melville, dream of goodness was not whollly impossible. Like Hawthorne, he did not diagnose the root cause of the failure of the dream in the inherent sinfulness of man. Rather, he showed man's helplessness being entrapped into moral ambiguities and victimised by his situation in life. *Billy Budd* unfolds that truth. Here the setting is a man-of-war where martial law snatches the democratic rights. Billy Budd, 'the natural democrat', being transhipped from the merchant ship. 'The Rights of man' to the warship 'Indomitable' lost his civil rights and had no freedom of will. This arbitrary decision of the ship's authority and black malice of the fellow mariners ultimately destroyed his inborn innocence. Captain Vere was well aware of the essential goodness of Billy Budd and believed he was 'innocent before God' and 'Nature'. Yet to maintain authoritarian discipline, specially at the time of mutiny, when martial law must prevail the Captain had to be loyal to the martial law and he condemned Billy tc death. This merciless operation of martial law is quite contrary to the natural law which owes its allegiance to instinct.

In *Moby Dick* Melville showed how democratic principles were voluntarily abdicated for following an evil purpose and ultimately described the superiority of natural law; whereas in *Billy Budd* he justified the operation of human law even at the cost of individual freedom.

Billy's calm acceptance of his tragic destiny showed how Melville "came to terms with the 'mystery of iniquity', content to acquiesce in what he could not, as no mortal can fully resolve",[23]

Billy Budd, which has been described as 'Melville's testament of acceptance', reveals Melville's rejection of democratic independence and an affirmation of the justice of established morality signifying the inevitable failure of the dream of freedom.

References

1. Robert and Spiller, *et al.* (eds.), *Literary History of the United States*, New York : Macmillan, 1960, p. 790.
2. *Ibid.*, p. 419.
3. Nathaniel Hawthorne, *The Scarlet Letter*, New York : Washington Square Press, Inc. 1960, p. 170.
4. *Ibid.*, p. 208.
5. *Ibid.*, p. 209.
6. *Ibid.*, p. 171.
7. F.O. Mathiessen, "The House of Seven Cables", A.N. Kaul (ed.), *Hawthorne: A Collection of Critical Essays.* (Twentieth Century Views) Englewood Cliffs, M.J., Prentice-Hall, Inc. 1966, p. 141.
8. Nathaniel Hawthorne, *The Blithedale Romance* (Introduction by Arlin Turner), New York: W.W. Norton Company, Inc. 1958, p. 37.
9. A.N. Kaul, "The Blithedale Romance", *Hawthorne: A Collection of Critical Essays,* pp. 154-55.
10. Hawthorne, *The Blithedale Romance,* pp. 28 and 40.
11. *Ibid.*, p. 46.
12. *Ibid.*, pp. 46-47.
13. A.N. Kaul, *Hawthorne: A Collection of Critical Essays,* p. 160.
14. Hawthorne, *The Blithedale Romance*, p. 224.
15. Robert and Spiller, *et al.* (ed.), *Literary History of the United States,* p. 437.
16 Hawthorne, *The Marble Faun* (ed. by Richard H. Rupp), New Delhi: Universal Book Stall, 1973, p. 419.
17. *Ibid.*, p. 166.
18. Newton Arvin, "Mardi, Redburn, White Jacket", Richard Chase (ed.), *Melville: A Collection of Critical Essays* (Twentieth Century

Views), Englewood Cliffs, N.J., Prentice-Hall, Inc, 1962, p. 22.

19. Newton Arvin, *Herman Melville,* London: 1950, p. 176.

20. Alfred Kazin, "Introduction to Moby-Dick", *Melville: A Collection of Critical Essays,* p. 47.

21. Marius Bewley, "Mellville and the Democratic Experience", *Melville: A Collection of Critical Essays,* pp. 106-07.

22. Alfred Kazin, "Introduction to Moby-Dick" *Melville: A Collection of Critical Essays,* p. 45.

23. Robert E. Spiller, *et al.* (ed.), *Literary History of the United States,* p. 469.

4

The Persistence of the Dream

BUT the dream persisted. The cleavage between the new ideas and old idealism reflected merely a change of mood and "no denial of the old faith but a new self-criticism directed toward practical effort".[1] So some of the writers in the later ages while criticizing the dream as vague and impossible, still cherished the ideals latent in it. Some of them cherished the dream for the sake of its beauty in contrast with the philistine reality of America. The indirect treatment and even the negative implications of the dream also signified the influence of the dream in the writings of the new era.

As in the nineteenth century, in twentieth century too the dream sometimes seemed to be admirable and desirable. The only difference was, the ideals of the dream were not always the same. So in Eugene O'Neill we find the romantic dream of beauty as an alternative to the American ideal of progress. Fugene O'Neill's characters sought after the beauty of the far off and the unknown, and the fountain of youth. He, along with his characters sharply reacted against the crude materialism of America and was in quest of the secret spot that nature has set apart from men and blessed with peace and harmony.

O'Neill's early plays affirmed the beauty of the dream in the sense of striving for an absolute perfection. But from the very beginning his characters instinctively felt the impossibility of realizing their ideals and they recognised the inevitable defeat of the dream. It seems they found the beauty of the dream in this very element of impossibility. From *The Long Voyage to The Fountain* his heroes preferred to die for their dream and remained true to their dream to the last. In pursuing their ideals they were doomed no doubt, but achieved a tragic greatness. Thus they exemplified "the great truth that there is nothing so precious in our lives as our illusions".[2]

But his dreamers mostly dreamed not of realization but of escape from the reality as a mark of protest against the sordid ugliness of American life. They rejected the American present and had no faith in the future too. His 'Yank' (*The Hairy Ape*), supposed to represent the typical American workingman, was painfully aware of his social inferiority. He dreamed of 'belonging' and wished for an ideal brotherhood. But like the earlier dreamers of perfection he too, found his peace being crushed to death in the arms of a caged ape whom he tried to hail as brother.

The question raised by Khan towards the end of *Marco Millions*: "The Word became their flesh, they say. Now all is flesh! And can their flesh become the Word again?"[3] Haunted the dramatist throughout his later plays. Realization of man's inability to perfect the materialistic society dominated by flesh, made him acquiescent. Accordingly he made his characters renounce the worldly happiness for restoring spiritual faith. So Lazarus strove for divine perfection and his failure embodied the impossibility of paradisial beauty. This led him to concern himself with the human imperfection. In *Strange Interlude* the dream turned to be a nightmare. Man is doomed by his own dream and so he remarked: "Romantic imagination ! It has ruined more lives than all the diseases ! Other diseases, I should say: It's a form of insanity!"[4] So Nina Leeds struggled for a compromise between the ideal and the actual.

Finally, Lavinia Mannon rejected the dream as a source of evil. *Mourning Becomes Electra* depicted the tragedy of man caused by man's own depravity. Lavinia accepted man's damnation resulting from the lust for baser things of life and discarded the dream of ideal beauty which fooled others. So at the end we hear her utter: "Tell Hannah to throw out all flowers."[5]

However, amidst the cheerless and frustrating reality of America, this dream of an impossible beauty, to O'Neill, was a source of great relief. Once he wrote to one of his friends. "The playwright of today must dig at the roots of the sickness of today as he feels it – the death of the old God and the failure of science and materialism to give any satisfactory new one for the surviving primitive, religious instinct to find a meaning for life in and to comfort its fears of death with."[6] He verily performed the duty of the playwright as prescribed by him in the above statement and dug 'at the roots of sickness of life' and found a 'meaning' in the philosophy of acquiescence.

Like Eugene O' Neill, John Steinbeck, too, was greatly inspired by the dream. Of course, his was not a quest for beauty, but for goodness and social progress. In him we find a fusion of transcendental mysticism and pragmatic realism. Like Emerson he was a preacher of oversoul and had faith in the common man. Again, like Whitman he dreamed of popular democracy to be attained through love for all. Along with these mystic beliefs and poetic ideas he combined a pragmatic view of how to make ideas effective in action. His characters tried to enact those old transcendental thought in the living reality and they embodied ideas in such a manner that no more did those seem to be mere abstractions. His characters did not wander on and on beyond the horizon to get lost. Rather they sought in reality a positive philosophy of life. So Jim Casy went to the wilderness not to escape from life but to reinvigorate the love for life by saving his soul in communion with nature. Being identified with nature he had the feeling of goodness and a holiness of spirit. He stated: "There was the hills, an 'there was me, an' we wasn't separate no more. We was one thing. In 'that one thing was holy'.[7] He had Emersonian conviction that holiness lies in the feeling of unity. Emerson, while discussing nature, pointed out that the world lacks unity because man is disunited with himself. Jim Casy had the similar feeling: "I got to thinking how we was holy, when we was one thing, an 'mankin' was holy when it was one thing."[8]

Steinbeck, in fact, found the modern evil in the possessive egotism of man and he was more afraid of this 'lust of spirit' rather than the 'lust of flesh'. "The quality of owning freezes you forever into 'I' and cuts you off forever from the 'We'."[9] So through Jim Casy he preached the religion of love to embrace and be the 'whole'. According to him everyman is an essential part of community and common good can be achieved through united effort of all – "May be all men got one big soul everybody's a part of."[10] This sums up his concept of oversoul. And once an individual is able to merge himself with the 'big soul' his own failure or death will be insignificant. As Tom said – "I'll be everywhere – whenever you look wherever they's a fight so hungry people can eat, I'll be there. Wherever they's a cop beating up a guy, I'll be there. . . . An 'when our folks eat the stuff they raise an' live in the houses they build – why, I'll be there. See'?"[11] To achieve social freedom and justice Steinbeck justified resistance to authority to become 'whole' in spirit. The hope of economic opportunity motivated his Okie's migration. Ultimately the hope proved to be futile. In his later novels this sense of defeat is pronounced. Yet Steinbeck affirmed his final faith in progress and dreamed of goodness of heart to ensure equal opportunity for all.

The strain of optimism is present in the writings of Sinclair Lewis, in his portrayal of grossly materialistic, money-mad America. His caustic satire directed against the grotesque vulgarity cannot suppress his sense of the promise of something better, something more fulfilling for the individual. Lewis the die-hard realist was a born romantic too. In him we find a curious blending of realism and romance. So his faithful depiction of the life in reality is pervaded with a note of happy optimism about the promise of American life.

In rejecting the charge of being "a raging reformer, an embittered satirist, a realist dreary as cold gravy" Lewis stated in an unpublished 'self-portrait': ". . . . In his stories Lewis does not happen to be amused only by the sea or midnight encounters on the Avenue, but oftener by the adventure of the soul in religion and patriotism and social climbing. . . ."[12]

Lewis's early heroes imbibed this spirit of adventure and looked for 'New Horizons'. They represented the potentiality of rebellion and heroism in the lives of 'little people' — a country boy, a timid clerk, a village girl. They embodied the conflict of cultural values and conflict of ideals with the reality of things. Following the nineteenth century tradition of 'realism' the early Lewis heroes found fault with the materialistic society and were eager to reform it. Carl Fricson, in *The Trail of the Hawk* had the glorious vision of brotherhood of man. Carl, the countryboy, rebelled against academic conventions and tried to be 'utterly tough and reckless' like a prairie radical to wander and discover. But his earlier ambition to reform society was swamped by the indomitable desire of becoming 'the best monoplane pilots America will ever see'. He lost himself on the glamorous adventure, the 'romantic and miraculous' aviation. Now he dreamed to become rich as soon as he could.' Being allured by the glamours of machine age Carl Fricson gave up his hope to reform society and rerurned to the very familiar world of economic security and social conventions.

Our Mr Wrenn also started with the theme of emotional education and spiritual emancipation. Mr. Wrenn, of course, was no dreamer or adventurer. Rather he was very much anxious to save his 'respectability', that is, his job in the Souvenir Company. But a small legacy freed the petty clerk from his economic servitude. The man who was previously so much afraid to lose his job and had imaginary adventures by means of steamship advertising brochures now left his job for a trip to Europe. This European adventure brought him in contact with Harry Morton, a socialist vagabond and Istra Nash, a cynical bohemian artist.

Istra introduced him to a wider world of art and culture and from Harry Morton he received a sense of that 'fine flame of shared hope' of socialism. These led him to a new discovery of America and Mr. Wrenn revolted against the very standard of 'respectability'. But his 'romance of culture' was short-lived. His experience of the world of art and intellect made him realize the significance of business world and like Carl Ericson he too became interested in self-advancement. His effort for spiritual emancipation was employed to raise his own status and he too returned to the native soil; for life in a Harlem flat was more romantic than travel in foreign lands.

Una Golden, heroine of the next novel *The Job* was an emancipated woman having faith in Utopian socialism – the recurrent early dream of Lewis's characters. "To Una there was no romance in the sick mansion, no kindly democracy in the village street, no bare freedom in the hills beyond."[13] The village girl was haunted by the vision of a better society and had the dual belief that "life is too sacred to be taken in war and filthy industries and dull education; and that most forms and organizations and inherited castes are not sacred at all".[14] She dreamed that "she would go to New York, become a stenographer, a secretary to Corporation President, a rich woman, free, responsible".[15]

So to be free and successful she left her known world and ventured for New York. But the 'loveless routine' of city life and the business world full of boredom and exhaustion made her disillusioned. She wanted to escape from the tedious jobs in the organizations operating on the principle"of giving the largest possible number of people the largest amount of nervous discomfort, to the end of producing the largest possible quantity of totally useless articles".[16] Finally, she had to make a compromise between her Job and Home.

Like Una Golden, Carol Kennicott too fled to New York and Washington in search of freedom and culture. She too was dissatisfied with her 'dull neighbours' having 'comfortable faith'.

She felt agitated by the ideas of the great world and wanted to experience the exotic images of beauty. She waged a war against prevalent philistinism. But the freedom which city life offered her was empty and her effort to reform the world was futile. Her interest in romantic personalities needed to be satisfied by her unromantic husband, Dr. Kennicott. Her return to Gopher Prairie was in fact, a return to reality suggesting the defeat of her idealism. But nevertheless, it implied the reaffirmation of her ideals. Carol Kennicott embodied Sinclair Lewis's challenge to the comfortable traditions and sure faiths of *Main Street* and his attempt to seek out "Whether there may not be other faiths."

Lewis the realist, as Rebecca West Calls him, was a 'fabulist' too. His *Babbitt* represented the archetypal American character, 'the standardised child of the standardised city' and introduced the cult of 'Babbittry'. He was the natural product of his society – the society where 'life at its most passionate is but a low grade infection': the society where men desire to get rich and women desire to rise socially. These men and women suffering from emptiness of soul and lack of integrity create a social void and lead a 'dehumanised life of utter indifference or enmity to all human values'.

George F. Babbitt the romantic, was unhappy withn his environments and longed for something better. He found nothing in life around which would serve as 'substitutes for joy and passion and wisdom'. He was befuddled in the human desert. Gradually he came to realize that all life as he knew and tried to live it was futile. He had not much pleasure out of making money and doubted about the worth to rear children merely that they might rear children who would rear children. He himself did not know what did he want. He sought relief in romance but received nothing nore than a momentary pleasure. To find remedy for the spiritual malady of his social group he rebelled against the conventions and supported the 'red' radicals. But that too he could not continue for long. His apprehension to be socially degraded forced him to return to the safe 'fortress of reality'. His sense of defeat was the natural outcome of the stultifying situation and the hostile environment yielding confusion of values and destruction of hopes.

Thus through repeated accounts of the heroes conforming to the realities of life and being victims of monstrous business culture. Lewis, in fact, emphasised the validity of idealism – the reminscence of nineteenth-century Utopianism. He was totally disillusioned with the current ideal of materialism. It seemed that the noble dream of Enlightenment – the ideal of progress and equality, faith in the excellence of life was gone. But through Martin Arrowsmith, the seeker of truth, Lewis proved that the faith of America is not dead. His quest for freedom is the 'adventure of the soul in religion and patriotism' for which he suffered an exile from social reality. Science was his new religion and like a true devotee he dedicated himself at the altar of scientific truth. He did never encourage the profiteering attitude of his materialistic society aiming to exploit science for ignoble causes. He cared for individuals, not for institutions. His concern for human welfare clashed with the commercial interest of the country and brought endless suffering to him. His passion for truth truimphed over the temptations for worldly success and finally he left the metropolitan life. Like Thoreau the Hermit, he took refuge in a cabin and as a true scientist worked hard to find out a new philosophy of life.

Of course, this idealism of Arrowsmith was renounced by *Ann Vickers*. Ann a feminist and social reformer lived a free life and searched for love in the midst of confusion of city life. But ultimately she chose to marry a man noted for dishonesty which meant the familiar divorce of life and ideals. Through her Lewis recognized the impossibility of attaining the ideals. However, his interpretation of American life in all its grotesque vulgarities is an indirect affirmation of the enduring spell of idealism.

The enthusiastic acceptance of dream as found in the works of Transcendental Optimists recur in the novels of Thomas Wolfe in the present century. His works re-echo the faith of the Declaration of Independence, Emersonian faith in the beneficent illusions of the universe and Whitman's celebrations of democracy. He discovered the 'promise of America' in 'the unkinged men' – the homeless wanderer, the lost people of the new world who struggle hard for sheer existence. Wolfe's was a quest for perfect democracy ensuring liberty and equality to everyman to live and work and to be himself.

In his earlier novels he pointed out the sharp contrast between 'two world discrete' – the aristocratic *Mannerhouse* and the democratic dream. He believed that ancestral tradition can give a man a mere 'good life' not the 'full life' for which he aspired. In reality one has to make a painful choice between these two and tradition played the dominant role as depicted in *Mannerhouse*. But in his next novel George Webber, the seeker of democratic ideals struggled hard to do away with the tradition. He searched for a 'full life' – full of both good and evil and to achieve this, he felt that he "... must unweave it from his brain, distil it from his blood, unspin it from his entrails."[17]

This 'unweaving' was tough job and he had to make a Faustian bargain of soul to the traditional devil. The world of reality was far away from the world of work, creative work. He wished to live in the world of creativity but not at the cost of flesh and blood reality. He founded his idealism on the rock of reality. He relied on the potentiality of the common people, the 'Men-Alive'. He admitted that "there is no greater wisdom than the wisdom of Eccelesiastes" and knew that "Man is born to live, to suffer, and to die, and what befalls him is a tragic lot."[18] Yet he was firm in his resolution not to accept this fatalism blindly,"but we Men-Alive, dear Fox, are right for Now. And it is for Now, and for us the living, that we must speak."[19]

Thomas Wolfe proclaimed his American faith in its fullest expression in *You Can't Go Home Again*. He searched for a way 'truer than facts' to realize the ideal democracy hidden in the actual one. He stated that all the real things like freedom, equal opportunity, and the integrity and worth of the individual which have belonged to the American dream since the beginning – they have become just 'words'. And his mission was to fulfil the dream in reality as to prove that freedom and equality were not just words but the 'real things'. The dream of perfection and progress are illusory no doubt, but Wolfe's heores believed this illusion to be true and lived for this illusion – this dream.

References

1. F. I. Carpenter, *American Literature and the Dream*, New York: Philosophical Library, Inc., p. 83.
2. A.H. Quinn, *Representative American Plays*, New York: 1928, p. 966.
3. "Marco Millions", *Nine Plays by Eugene O'Neill*, New York: The Modern Library, 1952, p. 297.
4. "Strange Intertude", *Ibid.*, p. 384.
5. "Mouring Becomes Electra", *Ibid.*, p. 867.
6. Eugene O'Neill, quoted from Robert G. Spiller, *et al.* (ed.), *Literary History of the United States*, New York: Macmillian 1960, p. 1246.
7. John Steinbeck, *The Grapes of Wrath*, Penguin Book, 1939, p. 76.
8. *Ibid.*, p. 76.
9. *Ibid.*, p. 91.
10. *Ibid.*, p. 34.
11. *Ibid.*, p. 385.
12. Sinclair Lewis, quoted from Mark Schorer (ed.), *Sinclair Lewis: A Collection of Critical Essays*, Englewood Cliffe, N.J.: Prentice-Hall, Inc., 1962, p. 48.
13. Sinclair Lewis, *The Job*, p. 19.
14. *Ibid.*, p. 29.
15. *Ibid.*, p. 41.
16. *Ibid.*, p. 57.
17. Thomas Wolfe, *The Web and the Rock*, p. 119.
18. *Ibid.*, p. 113.
19. *Ibid.*, p. 119.

5

The Jazz Age
The Age of F. Scott Fitzgerald

THE dream persisted, at least for sometime more, because World War I, made the world of 1920 richer and more comfortable to the millions of Americans. Indeed, it was Europe that had suffered most in the War and lay paralytic after four shattering years whereas America became merely disillusioned by the war. As Alfred Kazin remarked in his book *On Native Grounds*: "It was Europe that came out of the war only to enter upon the Fascist agony, where America now emerged completely as a dominant world Power."[1] The total atmosphere was full of gaiety and recklessness; America had a triumphant self-discovery which was echoed in the new literature of the period. For the first time the Americans, specially the younger generation – 'the famous younger generation that was to make history in the twenties' – felt a sense of release from the old orders of convention and puritanism. With the exhilaration of the sudden freedom there came a 'youthful perkiness' and in the heady world of the twenties the children of the boom in their growling dissatisfactions with the American society revolted against the parochial shelters and craved for new experiences. The young minds under the war-time pressure and the influence of continental manners felt the necessity of a new code which ultimately led to the breakdown of traditional restraints and taboos. Victorianism lost its hold and was 'parodied to death by the debunkers'. The attitude of the young people has been tellingly expressed by John F. Carter, "the older generation had certainly pretty well ruined this world before passing it on to us. They give us this thing, knocked to pieces, leaky, red-hot, threatening to blow up; and then they are surprised that we don't accept it with the same attitude of pretty decorous enthusiasm with which they received it, way back in the eighties."[2] F. Scott Fitzgerald, one of the central figures of this period, observed this great distrust of the youth when he said that the younger generation emerged from the war 'to find all Gods dead, all wars fought, all faiths in man shaken'.[3]

The post-War decade in America or the Jazz Age, as named by Fitzgerald, was significant for the rise of the youth. 'Everyone now seemed to belong to the Younger Generation, and the Younger Generation seemed to be everywhere".[4] The Jazz-band of the time tuned the Zeitgeist of the post-war age in its piercing music which was "endlessly sorrowful yet endlessly unsentimental with no past, no memory, no future, no hope".[5] The whole generation had been infected by the 'eat-drink-and-be-merry for tomorrow we-die spirit' and was floating on the time present. The war had transformed life by creating new opportunities. "The middle class public was distracted or indulgent, money was high, the literary business was booming, satire had become the order of the day, the custodians of orthodoxy seemed to be in retreat and a profligate culture refreshed itself on the legend of a rakish youth and the amusement of the new literature".[6] The modern spirit had finally come into power. The young intellectuals of the country – the 'civilized minority' – as called in *American Mercury* – rose in loud and bitter revolt. They felt the full disenchantment of the Peace of Versailles and became early converts to the devastating new psychology. For them, Freud promised a new West – virgin prairies of uninhabited impulse – and Neitzsche's anarchic individualism was a new version of Jeffersonian laissiez-faire. Freud and Nietzsche provided stimulus to the Bohemian minds to meet the challange of the new time by reflecting and interpreting its spirit, a spirit freely experimental, skeptical of inherited values. There was a revolt in their emotional and aesthetic world.

Fitzgerald, while naming the Age, explained how 'the word Jazz in its progress towards respectability has meant first sex, then dancing, then music'.[7] He observed further that a whole race was 'going hedonistic deciding on pleasure'. The generation about which Kazin remarked, 'no other generation in America ever seemed to have so radiant a youth', was thought by Fitzgerald to be "the wildest of all generations, the generation which had been adolescent during the confusion of the war, brusquely shouldered my contemporaries out of the way and danced into the limelight."[8]

This was a generation whose girls were dramatized as flappers and where 'the belle' had become the 'flirt', the 'flirt' had become the 'baby vamp'.[9] There was a 'real moral letdown' and a topsy-turvical change came into the realm of manners and morals. The young ones were keenly interested in adapting English customs to American conditions. The new moral code of that country, if it could be called a moral one at all, shocked the elders, who "stood firm wth all the stubbornness of the people involved in a weak case, preserving their righteousness and losing their children".[10] The young boys and girls had the fun of mixed parties in the curtained grills of speak-easies.

The 'petting-party', the popular phenomenon of the time, broke down the formidable barrier between the sexes. Boys and girls were permitted large freedom to dance and dine together with nominal chaperonage. The Victorian mothers were still thinking in their self-complacent moods that their daughters must look forward in innocence to a romantic love-match which would lead them to the altar and a happy living thereafter. They used to say, "*servant* girls are that way, . . . They are kissed first and proposed to afterward".[11] But to their astonishment the 'Popular Daughters' of the time with their short-hair and short-skirts were doing things, that even in a youngman's memory, would have been impossible: eating three "o' clock, after-dance suppers in impossible cafes, talking of every side of life with an air half of earnestness, half of mockery. . . ."[12]

In 1920 the *New York Times* reported about the dress of the flappers, that they had lifted their skirts 'far beyond any modest limitation' and they "rolled their stocking below their knees, revealing to the shocked eyes of virtue of fleeting glance of shinbones and knee-cap".[13] The boys in their turn liked to wear the hand-knit sleeveless jerseys which Amory, the cynical hero of *This Side of Paradise,* named as 'petting-shirts'. Their whole existence seemed to contain only sensuous music and dances – the dances which were described as 'syncopated embrace', by the editor of Hobart College Herald. "No longer did even an inch of space separate them, they danced as if glued together, body to body, cheek to cheek."[14] This new style of dancing was denounced in the religious journals of the day as 'impure, polluting, corrupting, debasing spiritually, increasing carnality' and it was thought that "the low-cut gowns, the rolled hose and short skirts are born of Devil and are carrying the present generations to chaos and destruction."[15]

Thus while the parents lay awake thinking whether their children were not utterly lost, the sons and daughters evaded questions or flared up to reply rudely that at least they were not dirty-minded hypocrites, that they saw no harm in what they were doing and proposed to go right on doing it. So the petting-parties became widely established 'as an indoor sports'. But "none of the Victorian mothers – and most of the mothers were Victorians – had any idea how casually their daughters were accustomed to be kissed."[16] Indeed, even at well-regulated dances the young folk used to retire in the darkened rooms or in the parked cars to engage in the unspeakable practice of petting and necking. The Jazz-babies like Rosalind in *This side of Paradise* could daringly confess that "I' have kissed dozens of men. I suppose I'll kiss dozens more."[17] The popular daughters wanted nothing but to be a 'speed' like Rosalind or Isabelle Borge.

However immoral and shocking it might have been, the elders thought, and hoped that with the coming of maturity this flare up of youth would be set right again. But they were mistaken in their views, because this revolt of the younger generation was only the beginning of a revolution of manners and morals that was already beginning to affect men and women of every age in every part in the country. Diverse factors worked in the backdrop to cause this upheaval and reversal of values in American life.

Then revolution was stimulated by the new status of women. The idea of 'women-liberation', the cry of the present times, had its origin in the early twenties. The American women obtained her franchise in 1920, which gave her altogether a new meaning in life. It consolidated her position as man's equal. With the achievement of political right, economic independence grew and economic independence in its turn created an urge in her for the independence from the drudgeries of housekeeping. The modern amenities provided by the improved scientific appliances reduced her domestic hardship and left a lot of time at her disposal to go into the world outside. She found jobs in offices of publishers and advertisers, in the departmental stores. The material world with all its momentary pleasures allured the women to have their own lives. No more could a woman be satisfied with being a wife and a mother only. She explored the forbidden land of self and indulged in amoral habits. In the words of Rosalind she could say,"I like sunshine and pretty things and cheerfulness – and I dread responsibility. I don't want to think about pots and kitchens and brooms. I want to worry whether my legs will get slick and brown when I swim in the summer".[18] The women of this decade worshipped merely youth, – 'unripened youth'. They acted as men's casual and light-hearted companions and irresponsible playmates. The women of the day promised men to give not the companionship of mature wisdom, but "the thrills of sex without their fruition. . . . And to herself she added. But I will be free."[19]

The influence of Sigmund Freud was no less a revolutionary element in changing the attitude of the American people. Though Freudian works were published in the nineteenth century and the

Americans listened to the lecture of Freud and Jung as early as 1909, yet it was only after the War had ended that the Freudian theory became the gospel of American life. The post-war America provided a very fertile ground for the seeds of Freudianism to grow rapidly and widely. Even from the lips of the flappers one could hear, "I'm hipped on Freud and all that, but it's rotten that every bit of real love in the world is ninety-nine per cent passion and one little *soupçon* of jealousy."[20] Sex appeared to be the central and pervasive force to which every human motive could be atrributed. Now words and terms like sadism. masochism, inferiority complex, Oedipus complex, Electra complex, etc., found place in American literature. It became a fashion for the intellectual ladies to go to Europe for being analysed. The custodians of orthodoxy preached self-control but the outspoken people thought it to be out-of-date.

The other forces which stimulated the revolution were prohibition, the automobile, sex magazines, and movies.

With the execution of Prohibition Act, the large cities of the North and East suddenly became full of bootleggers, the speak-easies and the cocktail parties. Drinking became the 'thing to do' in many communities. In this regard Allen commented that "Under the new regime, not only the drinks were mixed, but the company as well."[21] While attempts were being made to make Prohibition permanent, men and women were drinking together at the speak-easy bars and serving of cocktails before dinner became almost socially obligatory. During the weekends people started going out in automobiles with gin in their hip pocketrs and girls in their arms. Alcohol flowed more freely than ever before even among the under-graduates.

Automobile facilitated the means of being away from the watchful supervision of the parents and chaperons. To go on joyriding in the closed cars became a common experience. The report of the juvenile court quoted by the Lynds declared automobile to be a "house of prostitution on wheels".[22]

Finally the sex and confession magazines and movies made the revolution complete. Each of them had remarkable influence for developing the reactionary attitude of the people. The circulation of the magazines dealing in the stories of sex-adventure and confessions started towards 1919. The object of these magazines were simply to titillate the sensual cravings through frank descriptions about the secret of sex and juicy scandals.

To keep pace with the popularity of the magazines the producers of the movies too played incessantly upon the lucrative theme. The language in which they advertised their movies had erotic overtones: "brilliant men, beautiful jazz-babies, champagne baths, midnight revels, petting parties in the purple dawn, all ending in one terrific smashing climax that makes you gasp."[23] Though the pictures were not as promising as in the advertisement they were successful in arousing wild excitement in millions of spectators.

To sum up, the post-war disillusionment, the new status of women, the Freudian gospel, prohibition, automobiles, the magazines and movies – all these various factors transformed the existing order of the society and "the Jazz Age now raced along under its own power served by great filling stations full of money".[24]

The Jazz Age flowering in 1920 continued up to 1929. But from 1922 onwards – the peak year for the younger generation, the Jazz Age tended gradually less and less to be an affair of youth. This is how Fitzgerald describes this situation. "The sequel was like a children's party taken over by the elders leaving the children puzzled and rather neglected and rather taken aback."[25] The middle-aged persons over thirty, 'the people all the way up to fifty", joined the carnivals. Even in the small cities people were quick to adopt a new culture sprouting on the ruins of old conventions and ideals. The sober table had rturned into a gay one and as mentioned before, the virtue of celibacy became a past glory. "The gay elements of society had divided into two main streams, one flowing toward Palm Beach and Deauville and the other, much smaller toward the summer Riviera."[26] Americans were wandering in places like Russia, Persia, Abyssinia, and Central Africa. But Paris seemed to be more attractive than all. By 1928 Paris had grown suffocating with American citizens who were travelling in luxury. Paris became the 'chosen land' for the American expatriates because living in Paris was not only cheaper but it was more 'casual and open'. Hoffman thought that "The exodus from America was also a part of the strategy in fighting American Puritanism."[27] According to him puritanism could be blamed for overrating morality and suppressing art which resulted in the suppression of normal life "and finally (as a modern businessman) made both morality and art servants of financial success".[28] 'Macolm Cowley gave an amusing analysis of the general reaction against puritanism in his sketch 'Young Mr. Elkins'. Mr. Elkins 'being an American intellectual belongs to the professionally young'. To be free from 'American grossness and American puritanism' he worked out his own thesis. "Puritanism is bad; America is puritan; therefore America is bad."[29] The young Americans thought that America lacked taste and to free themselves from the crude, vulgar, pretentious taste that "crushed the sensitive soul, rewarded the unscrupulous and the thick skinned... "[30] wished to migrate from their native land.

Expatriation was partly an expression of Bohemainism and 'Any Bohemia is an expresion of the Utopian wish.' For the Americans the attraction of a 'second country' contained some element of Utopian wish; — "freedom from responsibility, a chance to criticize that world, and to make over one's life according to personal taste".[31] In the distortion of their new conditions, thus, expatriation in the Jazzy twenties sustained the American spirit and had a profound impact on the quality and the nature of the decade's life and art.

This revolutionary period however, was an uneasy time to live in. The new code of morals along with the new freedom was alluring and elusive. The Americans were in the pursuit of their dream of 'success' and 'money'. Being haunted by their 'dream' they sought after deceptive values in life. They made money no doubt, and America tested the fruits of Coolidge-prosperity. But strangely enough this very boom led to a widespread neurosis and sensitive minds, as Fitzgerald said, began 'to disappear into the dark maw of violence'. The moral catastrophe happened not during depression, but at the peak of prosperity; because it was not so easy to break with the traditional values of life overnight and the new code which was born in disillusionment persisted to be a disillusioning one for a decade and could not substitute the richness and the strength of old-ordered life. So the American Adam lay disenchanted and innocence started giving way to experience.

References

1. Alfred Kazin, *On Native Grounds*, New York; Harcourt, Brace and World, Inc. 1942, p. 190.
2. John F. Carter, "Atlantic Monthly", September 1920, quoted in F.L. Allen, *Only Yesterday*, New York: Bantam Books, 1931, p. 84.
3. F. Scott Fitzgerald, *This Side of Paradise*, New York: Scribner's 1970, p. 282.
4. *On Native Grounds*, p. 193.
5. *Only Yesterday*, p. 10.
6. *On Native Grounds*, p. 193.
7. F. Scott Fitzgerald, "Echoes of the Jazz Age", *The Crack-Up*, New York: New Directions Paperbooks, 1956, p.1.
8. *Ibid.*, p. 15.
9. *This side of Paradise*, p. 59.
10. *The Crack-up*, p. 16.
11. *This side of Paradise*, p. 58.
12. *Ibid.*, p. 59.
13. *Only Yesterday*, p. 79.
14. *Ibid.*, p. 80.

15. *Ibid.*, p. 82.
16. *This Side of Paradise*, p. 58.
17. *Ibid.*, p. 175.
18. *Ibid.*, p. 196.
19. *Only Yesterday*, p. 97.
20. *This Side of Paradise*, p. 238.
21. *Only Yeaterday*, p. 89.
22. *Ibid.* p. 89
23. *Ibid.*, p. 90.
24. *The Crack-up*, p. 18.
25. *Ibid.*, p. 15.
26. *Ibid.*, pp. 18-19.
27. Ferederick J. Hoffman, *The Twenties*, New York: Collier Books, 1962, p. 53.
28. *Ibid.*
29. Malcolm Cowley, "Young Mr. Elkins", quoted from *The Twenties*, p. 54.
30. *The Twenties*, p. 53.
31. *Ibid.*, p. 55.

6

This Side of Paradise
The Dawn of Experience

FITZGERALD'S fundemental attitude towards experience as revealed in his first novel *This Side of Paradise* is serious and moving. There is something of the intensity of deeply felt experience in it. He believed, as he said: "If you weren't able to function in action you might at least be able to tell about it, because you felt the same intensity – it was a backdoor way out of facing reality."[1] Accordingly all his best writings were written out of his own sense of experience with a desire to relieve and cope with his sense of hurt. He suffered a number of wounds at different phases of his life. While writing *This Side of Paradise* his mind was obsessed with some important events at that most delicate and sensitive stage of life; his failure to win the love of a golden girl like Ginevra King; his failure to get a Princeton degree; his romantic attitude towards the perils of war and finally Zelda Sayre's refusal to marry him since he was not rich enough. Bitter memories caused by these events as well as several false starts and unrealized plans haunted him and created a sense of despair in him which he tried to release through this fiction. Amory Blaine is almost a direct projection of the author himself and his image is developed in the ideal perfection of his egotism. Amory is the first Fitzgerald hero who enacts Fitzgerald's living experience of his own society and time.

This Side of Paradise presumed, among other things, to introduce a generation and to preside over its traumatic birth. Its hero, Amory Blaine, is a kind of *novus homo* of the twenties, the prototype of self-consciousness. The novel's order of progression is Amory's growth and gradual transformation from the son of a Victorian mother into what Fitzgerald calls an 'egotist', and then from egotist to 'personage'. The title 'personage' is most significant for Fitzgerald who uses it synonymously with individual, that is democracy's aristocrat – the newly-born self arrived at last when the threshold of life leads to some extraordinary human service. One must become a self before he can sacrifice self. But whatever Amory Blaine is, he is the essential self of Fitzgerald.

Fitzgerald's own experiences embodied the glamour as well as the sense of loss in the young generation of the wild twenties. Amory Blaine possessed his own imaginative innocence and youthful vision too. Along with his aristocratic pride and self-possession Amory was endowed with all the qualities of a romantic youth. Fitzgerald had a definite attitude towards youth. For him youth was a time of fresh energy and vitality – a time of promise and infinite possibilities – of expectation and abilities to create the platonic image of the self. Amory was created with this idealized concept of youth full of ambition and hopes and he was not satisfied with the mere association "with glittering things and glittering people – he wanted the glittering things themselves".[2]

Amory Blaine is a typical American youth – fresh, vital and innocent – aspiring to be great. His story is the story of the son of a Victorian mother gradually growing up first into a romantic egotist, then a personage and at last a personality. At the very outset he is an 'enchanted voyager' with 'penetrating green eyes' and 'a facile imaginative mind' when all things seemed larger than life and purer than dream.

The first few years of his life are spent in the idyllic and effeminate atmosphere where the shadow of his dominating mother instills in him an obsessive egotism, a dreamy sentimentalism and a romantic restlessness. In later years of his life this overwhelming presence of the mother is replaced by the other girls and women whose varying influence made him aware of evil and human suffering.

'From his fourth to his tenth year he did the country with his mother', 'deriving a highly specialized education from' her.[3] At the age of five 'he was already a delightful company for her' whose indulgence made him precoucious and overconfident. So at eleven only, he did not hestitate to sample with his mother's apricot cordial and 'essayed a cigarette in his exultation' which horrified his mother yet secretly amused her too. Beatrice, as he used to call his mother, often would be heard commenting before other ladies "This son of mine is entirely sophisticated and quite charming — but delicate. . . ."[4] This attribution *delicate* gives clue to Amory's character. His precociousness and a feeling of superiority complex could never suppress his freshness of mind and softness of heart. This delicacy of character had led him to many an emotional crisis.

During his stay at Minneapolis with his aunt and uncle "the crude, vulgar air of western civilization first catches him".[5] He was only thirteen then. He had the experience of kissing a girl for the first time in his life in the bobbing party of Myra of St. Claire. He imagined to like Myra most and flattered her so much that ultimately "Myra led the way into the little den of his dreams, where a cosy fire was burning before a big sink-down couch" which "was to be a great stage for Amory, a cradle for many an emotional crisis."[6] His great eagerness for romance made him talk romantically and act impulsively. But at the very moment when "their lips brushed like young wild flowers in the wind" a "sudden revulsion seized Amory, disgust, loathing for the whole incident".[6] Immediately he got disillusioned and was upset pervaded by a sense of sin and an unknown fear. "He desired frantically to be away, never to see Myra again, never to kiss any one"; and he wanted "to creep out of his body and hide somewhere safe out of sight, up in the corner of his mind".[7] This single incident clearly indicates his purity of mind and a sort of innocence as Adam had before his fall. The romantic egotist in him was totally different from this puritan innner self which he preserved to the end. Isabelle, Clara, Rosaland, Eleanor – all the girls whose love he sought at different times, made him more and more aware of this 'self' and later the 'problem of evil' for him 'solidified into the problem of sex'.[8]

Thus the mother's son slowly entered into the wider world and got involved in the complexities of life. Of course, he thought himself to be "a fortunate youth capable of infinite expansion for good or evil" and "assumed the most romantic of expressions and walked on the air-cushions that lie on the asphalts of fourteen".[9] 'One of his favourite waking dreams' at this time was "about becoming a great half back" or "the youngest general in the world". "It was always the becoming he dreamed of, never the being."[10] 'Aristocratic egotism' was his first philosophy, a code to live by. He had his own self-estimation. "Amory thought that he was exceedingly handsome. He was.... He granted himself personality, charm, magnetism, poise" and so on which made him consider himself to be somebody with an unquestioned superiority over others.[11] It may sound as his arrogance and vanity. True, he was suffering from a complex; but he had a Puritan conscience which made him feel at times that "he possessed neither courage, nor perseverance, nor self-respect". With this conflict in mind "did Amory drift into adolescence".[12]

Amory started his formal education at St. Regis Connecticut. Before he joined his classes he spent a week with Monsignor Darcy, once a young pagan, now turned into a very moral and religious clergyman. His brilliant and enveloping personality acted as the radiant sunlight to many people. Amory had a wonderful time with this friendly churchman who was actually adored by the children and the youth and liked most by the elders for his quality of "appreciating life to the fullest". His cheerful disposition and friendly discussion enlightened Amory – whose "mind turned inside out, a hundred of theories confirmed, and his joy of life crystallised to a thousand ambitions".[13]

Life at St. Regis for two years subdued the egotist in Amory to certain extent. He was "generally considered both conceited and arrogant and universally detested".[14] This made him resentful to those having authorities over him, indifferent to his study. Getting discouraged he associated himself with a few whom he could use 'as mirrors of himself'. But practically he was unbearably lonely and desperately unhappy. Years afterwards whenever he thought of St. Regis, he would picture himself "only as the unadjustable boy who had hurried down corridors, jeered at by his rabid contemporaries mad with common sense".[15] Though "he went all wrong at the start" in the last year at St. Regis, the football match with Groton made him feel the 'eternal hero' and taste the exciting joy of triumph. His status was raised further with the editorship of 'St. Regis Tattler'. He devoted himself to musical and lyrical outpourings and 'slumped into dreamy content'.

With the tide of time he was changed and "St. Regis had very painfully drilled Beatrice out of him, and had begun to lay down new and more conventional planking on the fundamental Amory".[16] But some of the basic traits in him for which he suffered were still unchanged. His moodiness, his tendency to pose, his laziness, and his love of playing the fool – all together indicated a sort of eccentricity in him. He formulated his theory on 'the slicker' a term chosen to refer to the well-dressed boys with a definite social position, 'wiser and shrewder than his contemporaries', always aspiring for the worldly success. Amory in his boyish ambition wished to be 'slicker'. But his secret ideal was to possess courage and tremendous brains and talents to lend further glory to the image conceived.

The next phase of Amory's life started at Princeton University where the egotist became an aesthete. Princeton attracted him with its atmosphere of bright colours and its alluring reputation as the pleasantest country club. "From the first he loved Princeton – its lazy beauty, its half-grasped significance, the wild moonlight revel of the rushes, the handsome prosperous big game crowds, and under it all the air of struggle that pervaded his class."[17] But he hated the existing "social barriers as artificial distinction made by the strong to bolster up their weak retainers"[18] and as he was the only boy from St. Regis he felt himself socially outcast. This class-distinction troubled his mind and made him frantically wish to be one of the 'gods of class' and he took to all the possible avenues lying open before him. His old dream of becoming an athlete inspired him to join the foot-ball game wherein the very first week he perceived a serious injury and was compelled to retire for the rest of season. Then he resorted to literary activities and wrote for *Nassau Literary Magazine*. All the while he was guided by the very desire 'to be admired', and sometime aspiring to reach even the envious position of the 'Princetonian Chairman' or 'Triangle President' to be one of the 'hot cats on top'. But all these new hopes and ambitious stirrings made him feel strengely alone and restless. "He tried hard to look at Princeton through the satiated eyes of Oscar Wilde and Swinburne."[19] Shaw, Chesterton, Keats, Pinero, Yeats and many others were included in his reading list and he was greatly influenced by Tom D'Invillers, one of his class-mates who already had earned fame as a poet. The spirit of the spires and towers made him dreamily acquiscent sometimes, and sometimes it 'overawed' him, and he could well realize his own inconsequnce and insufficiency.

After his freshman year the war began which failed to thrill or interest him. He was more concerned with Triangle Club activities like presenting a musical comedy and having shows at different fashionable cities. Now he had no time to feel bored and was in full stride, confident, nervous, and jubilant.

Triangle trip made Amory aware of the 'great current American phenomenon' the 'petting party'. He was shocked to see the girls in the fashionable cities between New York and Chicago doing impossible things that their Victorian mothers could never imagine. The 'Popular Daughters' were 'kissed first and proposed to afterward'. Amory saw them 'strut and fret in the lobby' having after-dance suppers in impossible cafes, "talking of every side of life with an air half of earnestness, half of mockery". Amory took all these things for 'a real moral let-down'. His puritan conscience made him see the cities as 'one vast juvenile intrigue'. But he could not save himself from being entrapped into this intrigue. Isabelle Borge, the 'Speed' attracted him so much that he decided to spend his holidays in Minneapolis instead of visiting his mother at home. Amory's lack of experience made him see in her eyes 'the light of the idealist', and she seemed to be 'the inviolate dreamer of Joan-like dreams' whereas in actuality her "flirt smiled from her large black-brown eyes and shone through her intense physical magnetism".[20] But Amory's personality was rather a mental thing. And so very soon he got disillusioned with Isabelle. Her arrogance hurt him and her coldness piqued him and he had no real affection for Isabelle though only a few days ago their romance 'seemed to both of them infinitely charming, infinitely new'. She had been nothing except what Amory read in her. She was just a popular daughter and simply played with his emotions and 'spoiled a year'. Amory's disillusionment, however, made him look at life from a new angle and he knew that 'his life would not be unfulfilled'.

Almost at the same time the accidental death of Dick Humbird gave a very hard blow to his highly sensitive mind and aroused a sense of futility in him. The cold, pale face of Dick haunted Amory's imagination and was associated with the sense of guilt for ever.

Amory's philosophpy of success tumbled down as a result of his failure in the examination leading to his removal from the Princetonian Board. Sudden death of his father and the consequent financial difficulties made the situation worse for him. His ambition for success through the gateway of wealth was badly affected.

In order to restore his lost spirit his mother entrusted him to the care of Monsignor Darcy as she herself could no more keep constant watch over him. Monsignor Darcy, indeed, was Amory's true friend, philosopher and guide. He loved Amory deeply and censored or consoled him at times whatever was necessary. He asked Amory to be a 'personage' and not a 'personality' since 'personality' according to him meant merely a physical matter which glitters and makes a man think himself to be very much important. But a person is what he does and not what he thinks to be. A man lives in his action only and a 'personage' is ever-active who always aims at to do *the next thing.* "He is never thought of apart from what he's done. He's a bar on which a thousand things have been hung – glittering things sometimes, . . . but he uses those things with a cold mentality back of them."[23] Amory felt inspired at this idea of becoming a 'personage and 'do the next thing'. Some of his glittering possessions had fallen off, but he decided to collect some new ones. He returned to college wishing to have a clean start and found the undergraduate body interesting. But very soon his encounter with the devil, first in the cafe, then in the girls' apartment did upset him very much and he had a sort of nervous breakdown. He came to himself only in the company of his friends and their discussions on various topics helped him to get back his spirit. "This sense of going forward in a direct, determined line had come back: youth was stirring and shaking out a few new feathers. He had even stored enough surplus energy to sally into a new pose."[22]

At this stage Clara Page came in his life adding a new significance to it. Fitzgerald wrote in a preface to the book about Amory, "The leading character loved many women, and gazed at himself in many mirrors."[23] This time too Clara in her ethereal and supernatural beauty presented a new mirror and Amory's narcissistic nature reacted accordingly. His preraphelite sensibility made him feel an ideal and aesthetic perfection in her beaming beauty and she appeared to him to be the daughter of the light. "He sees himself in front of her as Joseph before the eternal significance of Mary."[24] She was the only girl he ever knew who understood him well and estimated him correctly. "You're a slave, a bound helpless slave to one thing in the world, your imagination."[25] She made Amory confess that he adored and worshipped her more than he loved her. Amory fascinanted her but could not get her love. She had her 'precious babies' and to remain true to them she kept Amory out of her life.

Then came a shadowy period in his life with the sudden surge of war. "Amory realized poignantly that this was the last spring under the old regime."[26] He put the blame for the war on the ancestors of his generation. "War rolled swiftly up the beach and washed the sands where Princeton played" and Amory felt it caused them to leave their "whole heritage of youth" and break all the links that seemed to bind them "to topbooted and high-stocked generations."[27] War announced the beginning of an end and Princeton life closed with an elegiac note on the fleeting moment and the approaching dangers. Amory prepared himself for new trials to come and with a heavy heart started for an unknown future. A sense of loss overtook him. "No more to wait the twilight of the moon in this sequestered vale of star and spire, for one eternal morning of desire passes to time and earthly afternoon. Here, Heraclitus, did you find in fire and shifting things the prophecy you hurled down the dead years; this midnight my desire will see, shadowed among the embers, furled flame, the splendour and the sadness of the world."[28]

The interlude followed. War made Amory separate from his friends and his moral guardian Monsignor Darcy. In the meanmtime he lost his mother too. Amory could not decide what he would do if at all he was to survive that war. Sometime he conjectured that being an educated man he ought to join politics; since he felt that in those days politics in the U. S. A. was left to the 'muckers'. At some other time he wished that "he would write immortal literature if he were sure enough about anything to risk telling any one else about it."[29] In a letter to his friend Tom D' Invillers he wrote: "I confess that the war instead of making me orthodox, which is the correct reaction, has made me a passionate agnostic."[30]

"I hope something happens" – this expectation haunted him and made him 'restless as the devil'. This restlessness led him to another emotional crisis which shattered his romantic illusion further. War could not destroy his buoyancy and he still cherished his romantic aspiration to get the most beautiful girl in life. Rosalind was his new mirror' "no polite mirror, to reflect the handsome image but a polished stone that darkens the reflection".[31] Rosalind was typical of her generation who 'had great faith in man as a sex' and her own younger sister Cecilia commented on her, "you want life to be a chain of flirtation with a man for every link".[32] Her bewitching beauty deceived Amory easily and very soon he took her to be his life and hope and happiness. His deep love for her made him forget his financial condition, that he was drawing thirtyfive dollars a week only and doing a petty job in an advertising company. Since he had no money, he had no status, – specially in the eyes of Rosalind and her mother who cared for money only. Amory in his youthful imagination, on the contrary, dreamed to marry Rosalind and he happy thereafter. But Rosalind did not accept this mere 'dreamer'; she just played on with his emotions and rejected him in favour of Dawson Ryder whose wealth gave him a better background and strengthened his position as a suitor. Rosalind wanted affluence of wealth to give her 'sunshine and pretty things and cheerfulness' and knew that Amory with his mere 'love', however passionate that might be, could give nothing. While Amory for the sake of his love was preparing to shoulder responsibility, Rosalind, on the other hand, denied to bear any burden of love. Her rejection caused the long bitterness in Amory and made his life empty: "She had taken the first flush of his youth and brought from his unplumbed depths tenderness that had surprised him, gentleness and unselfishness that he had never given to another creature."[33]

To shield himself from the stabs of memory he took resort to drinking and his drunken sprees destroyed the image of Narcissus in him. His 'experiments in convalescence' marked the beginning of his inner growth. "He was emotionally worn-out. The people and surroundings that he remembered as being cool or delicately artificial, seemed to promise him a refuge."[34] His flight from reality to literature provided him some relief. He read enormously and started writing in order to come to terms with his own experience and reconsider his whole life. His problem was how to fit in and make use of his life for a greater cause. Though his own life was more devastated by his love affairs than war, yet from the gereral point of view Amory believed that war had ruined the old backgrounds and 'killed individualism'. He and his friends had to fight in the new frontiers of life.

As before, he sought for Monsignor Darcy's help and advice and accordingly he set off southward to join him in Washington. But as an irony of fate, he could not meet him and so decided to spend a few days with an ancient remembered uncle in Maryland where 'he lost a further part of him that nothing could restore'. The 'fundamental Amory' of his self, passionately desiring for adventure was still alive and his 'imagination ran riot' with Eleanor Savage, with the same old hope to get true love. Again the "evil crept close to Amory under the mask of beauty, the last weird mystery that held him with wild fascination and pounded his soul to flakes."[35] Beauty, specially the beauty of woman was 'inseparately linked with evil' in Amory's life. Again and again he was enchanted and betrayed by it. Everytime "he had reached toward it longingly it had leered out at him with the grotesque face of evil."[36] Eleanor who professed to be 'Psyche, his soul' and took Amory as her 'Juan', appealed to his literary moods. He found something most passionate in Eleanor's soft voice, a sort of 'weired chant'. Eleanor served a contrast to Clara. She played the role of the archetypal dark woman in Amory's life symbolizing the complexities of experience. She had a 'crazy streak' and in their 'last ride together' a kind of divine folly deranged her mind and their relationship came to a sudden end and both of them started hating each other with a bitter sadness. "But as Amory had loved himself in Eleanor, so now what he hatred was only a mirror", and the break with his narcissistic love was complete.[37]

In the following chapters we find Amory Blaine "in an eddy again, a deep lethargic gulf, without desire to work, to write, love or dissipate."[38] He seemed to be detached from his former self and risked his own social respectability in a gratuitous act of supercilious sacrifice. To honour his old friendship with Alec Connage and save his friend's public image he pledged his own prestige and allowed himself to be discredited in public. Then there was the public announcement of Rosalind's engagement with Dawson Ryder. Until now he had a secret hope, deep in his heart, that someday Rosalind might realize her mistake and 'would need him and send for him'. But from now onwards, for him she was dead. Almost at the same time sudden death of Monsignor Darcy completed the series of 'the collapse of several pillars'.

While attending Monsignor Dercy's funeral he realized that how much 'necessary' Monsignor had been to the people and what a sense of security he gave them. His cheerfulness and srtrength of mind was a good support for them to lean upon. This realization made Amory inspired and "he found something that he wanted, had always wanted and always would want – not to be admired, as he had feared; not to be loved, as he had made himself to believe; but to be necessary to people, to be indispensable."[39] He discovered himself newly and being liberated from egotistical complacency he gained a sense of humanity. His desire to be necessary to the people and give them a sense of security indicated his urge for socialism. His long monologues are marked with revolutionary zeal and his thoughts reflect the prevalent ideas on classless society. His past experience made him sharply react to the moneyed class and wish 'every boy ought to have an equal start'. He began to believe "that however the brains and abilities of men may differ, their stomachs are essentially the same".[40] He thought 'socialism' to be the only 'panacea'. He had an outburst of feeling towards the problem of disintegration faced by his restless generation. He was 'sick of a system where the richest man gets the most beautiful girl' and the artist has to sell his talent to the brutality of wealth as he himself had experienced. While emphasizing socialism Amory stressed the necessity of having faith in the traditional basic values of life. He knew 'faith is difficult'. But he realized that: "If living isn't a seeking for the grail it may be a damned amusing game."[41] For him, significance of life was a continuous search for faith and identity. He was at his journey's end now. He reached a definite goal – that is self-knowledge. His various struggles brought him ultimately the faith in himself which was uncrystallized before. So he found his true forte in his strong faith in the 'self' – the self ready to serve the people – a sort of religion embracing the humanity as a 'traditionary bulwark against the decay of morals'.

The romantic egotist and the aesthete in him gradually turned out to be a 'personage', a moralist. He lost his youth, lost his love but gained in something positive, something definite – the love of life. He was disillusioned, no doubt. All his romantic aspirations were gone and wishful thinkings died too. His experiences made him wise and initiated him "to help in building up the living consciousness of the race". He found his generation to be "a new generation dedicated more than the last to the fear of poverty and the worship of success; grown up to find all Gods dead, all wars fought, all faiths in man shaken. . . ."[42] He belonged to this generation, yet his faith in life kept him above since he gained in wisdom through loss and isolation.

"Amory was alone – he had escaped from a small enclosure into a great labyrinth. He was where Goethe was when he began Faust."[43] He stood alone at the threshold of experience and self-identity. Loss and isolation sharpened his melancholy into devotion. Life opened up in one of its amazing bursts of radiance and Amory stretched out his arms to the crystalline, radiant sky and proclaimed 'I know myself'.[44]

Amory paid for his knowledge with his youth and learnt the truth that one has to pay an atrocious price for the adventures in life. *This Side of Paradise* conveys this painful realization of the youth and his sense of regret about the loss of possibility and the end of expectation. But it also puts emphasis on the desire of Amory as well as of his author himself to relive the past. So

Fitzgerald made Amory say, "I regretted my lost youth when I only envy the delights of losing it. Youth is like having a big plate of candy. Sentimentalists think they want to be in the pure, simple state they were in before, they ate the candy. They don't. They just want the fun of eating it all over again. The matron doesn't want to repeat her girlhood – she wants to repeat her honeymoon. I don't want to repeat my innocence. I want the pleasure of losing it again."[45]

The significance of Amory's character lies not so much in his ideas but in his quest for self-knowledge which made him apart from and a superior to a philistine society. The 'self' he knows at last is the self of an artist which cannot be bound by any restriction and represent the sensitive soul trapped in the world of limitations. In his realization of Utopian aspects of dream and recognition of the value other than his generations he emerged as a conscience of his age and presumably dedicated himself to the sacred duty of writer and *This Side of Paradise* is the story where he writes of himself. Amory, the dreaming boy, was born anew into a disenchanted man aware of the meretriciousness of expectation, the pitfall of his own and his generation. He believed that though money is a necessary evil, yet it is not "the only stimulus that brings out the best that's in a man, even in America".[46] His very desire to attach a positive value to life distinguishes him from the reckless jazzy twenties and made him confidently announce, "I have neither been corrupted nor made timid by contemporary experience."[47] He remained innocent without living in innocence.

Fitzgerald said of himself that his was a 'New England conscience' raised in Minnesota. His fictional character, mid-West born, Minnesota raised Amory too, had rather a Puritan Conscience. It is this conscience that shapes their vision of reality and prepares them for a series of disillusionment, and more and more of experience. And that is why Amory could say boldly "I possess the most valuable experience, the experience of the race."[48] His experience has been a kind of birth trauma of a new self.

This Side of Paradise ends thus with a thrust into the future. Fitzgerald, succeeded in creating a new definition of individualism in contrast to the individualism of the genteel tradition. Amory Blaine arrived at his new form of individualism with a more responsible commitment to a social order. He had knocked away all his props of social place and social conventions and found a new and firmer foundation within himself. "He felt that he was leaving behind him his chance of being a certain type of artist. It seemed so much more important to be a certain sort or man".[49] Self-understanding and an ingrained moral sense give a new significance to Amory's character. His education through pain and suffering liberated him from dreamy sentimentalism and egotistical complacency. In his disillusionment he was born anew to recognize the values other than of his generations. Amory, like his author, tried to examine and evaluate his own self as well as the life he represented with an alien's remoteness and astonishment.

His rebelliousness was not without a sense of morality; when he repudiated the shallow conventions of society he also showed his inclination for a moral stability. In this respect this earlier creation foreshadows the mature works of Fitzgerald.

This Side of Paradise records in the accurate terms of intellectual honesty a reflection of American undergraduate life. It reveals the delightful experiences as well as the tribulations of the sensitive mind growing up in the changed atmosphere of the post-war society. It reflects the tension in the existing social order caused by an ideological commitment to the independent individual will and a practical desire for individuals to submit to social conventions and control. It reproduces the moment of transition from one generation to another and shows a radical change of attitude among the young. Immediately after publication of this novel Fitzgerald was greeted as the herald of a new age and the book was acclaimed as a book of protest and revolt in the name of liberty as a generic principle. The book seemed to advocate freedom from money, from bourgeois morality, from Victorian hypocrisy, from religion and from conformity. It shattered the idols, prejudices and lies of a society and tried to examine the social conventions. In the society in which anti-prohibition feelings, discussion of women's suffrage and emancipation, and Freudian theories were becoming popular, Fitzgerald's novel with its open references to 'petting and neckings', the unconventional behaviour of 'egotist's and debutantes naturally created a sensation. Fitzgerald's denunciation of the vulgarity of the new rich, his social criticism and his disarming frankness made him the spokesman of the younger generation – the generation that "bore him up, flattered him and gave him more money than he had dreamed of simply for telling people that he felt as they did. . . . "[50] He believed: "no one else could have written so searchingly the story of the youth of our generation".[51] Indeed, his concern for social realism made *This Side of Paradise* serve till today as a significant document of the post-war generation.

But the book is not merely a social history, it is a novel of deep and ingenuous emotions. Amory Blaine represents the curious and ambitious self of the (American) youth with freshness of feeling and earnest faith in romantic love. In portraying him Fitzgerald does not report but imaginatively recreates his experience – the experience of gradual development of a young man's emotional readiness for life. As a result, the objects, the people, the events and the convictions in context of which Fitzgerald develops the character of Amory are very much American and of his time. But his imagination works profoundly to bring forth a romantic attitude disciplined by his awareness of goodness and evil of human experience. Even at this very beginning of his literary career he had a kind of instinct for tragic view of life. Fitzgerald, later remarked about this fundamental trait of his imagination: "All the stories that came into my head had a touch of disaster in them – the lovely young creatures in my novels went to ruin, the diamond mountains of my short stories blew up, my millionaires were as beautiful and damned as Thomas Hardy's peasants".[52] Further, he wrote in his notebooks, "Taking things hard from Ginevra king to

"Joe Mank, that's (the) stamp that goes into my books so that people can read it blind like Braille".[53] *This Side of Paradise* though written at a quite young age makes an attempt to give expression to this essentially tragic vision of Fitzgerald.

This Side of Paradise went through two incomplete drafts before acquiring its final form. The first draft was completed at the end of Fitzgerald's college years and given to Christian Gauss who refused to send it to a publisher. The second draft known as "The Romantic Egotist" was completed at Fort Leavenworth, Kansas, in 1918 and sent to the publisher. But it was returned to him for revision. And finally the changed version of the novel came out under its present name in March, 1920. In the novel the whole subject-matter is divided into two parts separated by an interlude. The first part retains the title of "The Romantic Egotist", while the second bears a title, "The Education of a Personage". The story is told in the third person form of narrative, but the point of view except in a few cases, remains that of the young hero. The narrative voice alternates between the form of a soliloquy and the form of a dramatic monologue. In the first part the portrait of the hero is a direct projection of the author himself and is contemplated in the ideal perfection of his egotism. In the second part the protagonist is carefully developed through an education. Of course, this second part develops hints and germs already present in the first. But it centres on the thematic development of the episodes and the inner development of the character. In this connection, one may mention that action is dominated by characterization. However, the general tone of the work is more unified than the episodes in two parts. And if the theme – the theme of gradual humanization of Amory – is not properly focused and suffers from inconsistency, that may be attributed to author's inexperience and his inability to organize the material. Moreover, the novel has no unity of form. A purely dramatic interlude alternates with a descriptive sketch and a descriptive sketch in turn develops into pure dialogue. Letters and reading lists are inserted in the text, without sufficient reason; poems and songs, summaries and interludes, sensational openings and documentary reports are set out one against the other. In short, the book suffers from immature craftsmanship.

But after all this is the first novel and the author is still in the phase of literary apprenticeship. Despite the immature craftsmanship the book bears the evidence of Fitzgerald's possession of the gift that John Peale Bishop described as the rare faculty of being able to experience romantic and ingeneous emotions and a half hour later regard them with satiric detachment. Thus the novel, though lacking in artistic worth does not fall short of sincere and honest account of the artist's experience. No doubt, it has its faults. Even a critic like Edmund Wilson, whom Fitzgerald regarded as his 'intellectual conscience', vehemently criticized the book. To quote him: "*This Side of Paradise* is really not about anything; intellectually it amounts to little more than a gesture – a gesture of indefinite revolt. For another thing *This Side of Paradise* is very immaturely imagined: it is always just verging on the ludicrous. And finally, it is one of the most illiterate books of any merit ever published.... It is not only ornamented with bogus ideas and faked literary references but it is full of English words misused with the most reckless abandon".[54] Remembering this remark of Edmund Wilson, Fitzgerald commented much later in his life: "A lot of people thought it was a fake and perhaps it was, and a lot of others thought it was a lie, which it was not".[55] Here we may refer to Arthur Mizener's judgment on the book which is perfectly just. Mizener pointed out: "Fitzgerald's judgment and technique are inadequate almost everywhere in the book, but the fundamental alsmost instinctive attitude toward experience which emerges even at times through the worst of the book's surface, is serious and moving".[56] Though he agrees with Edmund Wilson that *This Side of Paradise* is in many ways a very bad book, yet he does not fail to see the merit of it lying in "the intensity of felt experience" that is so much in the language of Fitzgerald's mature books. According to him beneath all the author's naive earnestness about the romantic cynicism and philosophizing of Amory – one feels something of the 'real suffering of unhappiness'. In spite of all his dissections, Edmund Wilson too admitted that the book 'does not fail to live'. The book lives because of its youthful freshness and emotional exuberance. It is animated with graceful and vivid prose – sweet and modulated, light and harmonious. The powerful moving prose of young Fitzgerald could derive admiration from Gertrude Stein who proclaimed him "the only one of the younger writers who wrote naturally in sentences".[57]

A few illustrations will show how the young writer excelled in bringing out the varying emotions with superb ease and grace. The prose can be melancholy and dreamy in some sentimental moments:

> The last light fades and drifts across the land – the low, long land, the sunny land of spires; the ghosts of evening tune again their lyres and wander singing in a plaintive band down the long corridors and trees; pale fires echo the night from tower top to tower: Oh, sleep that dreams, and dream that never tires, press from the petals of the lotus flower something of this to keep, the essence of an hour. (*TSP*, p. 168)

Or it may denote the sense of sudden change and death creating an eerie atmosphere:

> So the grey car crept nightward in the dark and there was no life stirred as it went by. . . . As the still ocean paths before the shark in starred and glittering waterways, beauty-high, the moon-swathed trees divided, pair on pair, while flapping nightbirds cried across the air. . . .
>
> A moment by an inn of lamps and shades, a yellow inn under a yellow moon – then silence, where crescendo laughter fades . . . the car swung out again to the winds of June, mellowed the shadows where the distance grew, then crushed the yellow shadows into blue. . . . (*TSP*, p. 94)

Again it may be intensely sentimental, reminiscing and self-analytical too:

> There were days when Amory resented that life had changed from an even progress along a road stretching ever in sight, with the scenery merging and blending, into a succession of quick, unrelated scenes – two years of sweat and blood, that sudden absurd instinct for paternity that Rosalind had stirred; the half-sensual, half-neurotic quality of this autumn with Eleanor. He felt that it would take all time, more than he could ever spare, to glue these strange cumbersome pictures into the scrapbook of his life. (*TSP*, p. 250)

The beauty of Fitzgerald's prose style comes from his feeling for poetry. Much later he wrote to his daughter, "The talent that matures early is usually of the poetic, which mine was in large part".[58]

Scott Fitzgerald felt that the young writer must listen to that voice within that encourages him to record his feelings and actions because these feelings and actions are actually "his style, his personality – eventually his whole self as an artist".[59] Developing individuality is so very important that it is natural for the young writer, who has not yet acquired the tricks of interesting people because of lack of pattern or technique, to start with emotions that are close to him and that he can understand. The writer must 'sell his heart' his 'strongest reactions'. In a letter to Miss Frances Turnbull Fitzgerald expressed his convictions that all writers inevitably exploit their own emotions and experiences. He wrote: "It was necessary for Dickens to put into *Oliver Twist* the child's passionate resentment at being abused and starved that had haunted his whole childhood. Ernest Hemingway's first stories *In Our Time* went right down to the bottom of all that he had ever felt and known. In *This Side of Paradise* I wrote about a love affair that was still bleeding as fresh as the skin wound on a haemophile." (*Letters*, pp. 577-78)

Thus *This Side of Paradise* announces the major theme of Fitzgerald's total work. The novel reveals that Fitzgerald had an early grasp of his essential material although he had not yet learned to exploit it expertly. He naively exposed his themes before his increased sophistication shaped his insights into the more impressive configurations of *The Great Gatsby* and *Tender is the Night*. In Amory Blaine we can see the child who is father of the later men and in his dilemmas we find the compelling themes of Fitzgerald's work. The novel, in its quest for order and purpose and self-identity, clearly indicates the potentialities of Scott Fitzgerald to emerge as a serious and conscientions artist.

References

1. F. Scott Fitzgerald, *Afternoon of an Author*, New York: Scribner's 1958, pp. 185-86.
2. F. Scott Fitzgerald, "The Winter Dreams", *The Stories of F. Scott Fitzgerald*, (Introduction by Malcolm Cowley), New York: Scribner's, 1951, p. 130.
3. F. Scott Fitzgerald, *This Side of Paradise*, New York: Scribner's, 1970, p. 4.
4. *Ibid.*, p. 5.
5. *Ibid.*, p. 8.
6. *Ibid.*, p. 13.
7. *Ibid.*, p. 14.
8. *Ibid.*, p. 280.
9. *Ibid.*, p. 17.
10. *Ibid.*, pp. 17-18.
11. *Ibid.*, p. 18.
12. *Ibid.*, p. 19.
13. *Ibid.*, p. 26.
14. *Ibid.*, p. 27.
15. *Ibid.*, p. 36.
16. *Ibid.*, p. 32.

17. *Ibid.,* pp. 42-43.
18. *Ibid.,* p. 43.
19. *Ibid.,* p. 51.
20. *Ibid.,* p. 63.
21. *Ibid.,* p. 104.
22. *Ibid.,* p. 136.
23. Sergio Perosa, *The Art of F. Scott Fitzgerald,* Ann Arbor: The University of Michigan Press, 1969, pp. 19-20.
24.. *Ibid.,* p. 20.
25. *This Side of Paradise,* p. 143.
26. *Ibid.,* p. 152.
27. *Ibid.,* pp. 147, 153.
28. *Ibid.,* p. 154.
29. *Ibid.,* p. 162.
30. *Ibid.*
31. Sergio Perosa, *The Art of F. Scott Fitzgerald,* pp. 20-21.
32. *This Side of Paradise,* p. 172.
33. *Ibid.,* p. 209.
34. *Ibid.*
35. *Ibid.,* p. 222.
36. *Ibid.,* p. 280.
37. *Ibid.,* p. 240.
38. *Ibid.,* p. 245.
39. *Ibid.,* p. 266.
40. *Ibid.,* p. 275.
41. *Ibid.,* p. 278.
42. *Ibid.,* p. 282.
43. *Ibid.,* p. 264.
44. *Ibid.,* p. 282.
45. *Ibid.,* p. 258.
46. *Ibid.,* p. 273.

47. *Ibid.*, p. 277.
48. *Ibid.*
49. *Ibid.*, p. 81.
50. F. Scott Fitzgerald, "The Echoes of the Jazz Age", (ed. by Edmund Wilson), *The Crack-Up*, New York, New Directions Paperbook, 1945, p. 13.
51. F. Scott Fitzgerald, Letters p. 103.
52. F. Scott Fitzgerald, *The Crack-Up*, p. 87.
53. F. Scott Fitzgerald, Notebooks, *The Crack-Up*, p. 180.
54. Edmund Wilson, "Fitzgerald before The Great Gatsby", Alfred Kazin (ed.), *F. Scott Fitzgerald: The Man and His Work*, New York, Collier Books, 1966, p. 79.
55. F. Scott Fitzgerald, *The Crack-Up*, p. 88.
56. *Ibid.*, p. 30.
57. *Ibid.*, p. 308.
58. *Ibid.*, p. 305.
59. F. Scott Fitzgerald, quoted by John Kuehl, "Scott Fitzgerald's Critical Opinions", *Modern Fiction Studies,* Vol. VII, No. 1, Spring 1961, p. 15.

7

The Beautiful and Damned

The Broken Lute

FITZGERALD was faithful to his own experience and vision of the world and he tried his best to express the same in his own characteristic way. His second novel *The Beautiful and Damned* took him a step forward towards attaining maturity in thought as well as style. He himself had become wiser through his past experiences. The publication of *This Side of Paradise* took him to the peak of success and fulfilled his early ambitions. He won his golden girl and they both enjoyed the 'greatest and gaudiest spree'. But amidst his early success and abundance in life he could not forget the past humiliation and suffering and was haunted by the foreshadow of grim future. In reality, though much later, his apprehension became true. The tragic end awaited them both – Zelda a long term prisoner in mental asylum and he wasting his talent and money over reckless living.

In his new novel he studied and developed the character of Anthony Patch and his wife Gloria on the basis of his deep imaginative insight as well as the experience he had gained and the action in the novel is based on the development of characters. The development is of course, a negative one being a process of rapid distintegration and final decay. Fitzgerald wrote about this novel in a letter. "My new novel called *The Flight of the Rocket,* concerns the life of one Anthony Patch between his 25th and 33rd years (1913-21). He is one of those many with the tastes and weaknesses of an artist but with no actual creative inspiration. How he and his beautiful young wife are wrecked on the shoals of dissipation is told in the story."[1] Fitzgerald the moralist was in a problem to justify the eternal insertia inherent in the romantic self of the young protagonist, Anthony Patch, who the author says was his 'worry'. His story is the story of a journey from the golden illusion to the abyss of utter dissipation.

The story of the young artist is not the continuation of the story of Amory Blaine; it rather deals with the theme of deterioration and presents 'character in decay'. Anthony serves a sharp contrast to Amory. While Amory represents the growth of a personage full of ineradicable capacity of hope and emotional readings for life, Anthony with his lethargy and reluctance or work, disdain for labour and incapacity for hope, portrays the destruction of a personage. If Amory embodies the mystique of the artistic self-creation and significance of life, Anthony reveals an overall dissipation and meaninglessness of life. He stands at the door of the new age with his sensibility and longing but lacks in direction or purpopse. His hope without energy, ambition without effort make him drift in pointlessness. He can never reach the envisioned state of ideal love and happiness. The rocket-ride is downstrip only indicating a sharp moral decline. His distrust in the past and inactivity in the present destroys the possibility in the future. His very attempt to evade reality and live in the ivory tower of romanticism yields him nothing but misery and suffering. Ultimately he is dragged to the very core of reality and experiences the dark and grim apects of life. Inheritance of legacy denotes his spiritual bankruptcy. Squandering of all resources both physical and moral ruins his inner self and makes him the victim of 'jazz-age melancholia'.

Anthony Patch is presented as a thoroughly sophisticated young aesthete, independent and rich, enjoying the social security from being the grandson of Adam J. Patch the venerable philanthropist. His grandfather's illness (he has lost his parents long back) makes him live in his New York apartment and postpone his programme of living permanently abroad until his grandfather's death. Anthony eagerly awaits 'some golden day' when he would inherit 'many millions' and be able to perpetuate a carefree life. He dreams of that golden future and spends time leisurely in youthful imagination. His favourite retreat is the bathtub where he contemplates on sensual beauties – "He felt that if he had a love he would have hung her picture just facing the tub so that, lost in the soothing steamings of the hot water, he might lie and look up at her and muse warmly and sensuously on her beauty."[2]

But his puritan grandfather for whom strict morality and punctuality was 'the direct and primary cause of success' is very much dissatisfied with this idle way of living of Anthony. He asks Anthony 'to accomplish something', 'to do something'; and Anthony expresses his desire to write the history of the Middle Ages which makes Senior Patch scornful and he doubts whether Anthony really intends to work at all. Indeed, Anthony does nothing and, in fact, he detests "the notion of sitting down and conjuring up, not only words in which to clothe thoughts, but thoughts worthy of being clothed – the whole thing was absurdly beyond his desire".[3]

Feeling assured by the prospect of inheriting a great fortune he spends his time idly in the company of his selected friends and pays occasional visits to his grandfather as he does to his broker or tailor. If he feels bored he tries to get some diversions in Geraldine who "was company, familiar and faintly intimate and restful. Further than that he did not care to experiment – not from any moral compunction but from a dread of allowing any entanglement to disturb what he felt was the growing serenity of his life".[4] Geraldine acts as a mirror in which he can look at his own image from a distance (Narcissistic trait in Anthony as in Amory) but he cannot save himself from the bewitching beauty of Gloria Gilbert. She appears in his life as a dangerous incarnation of beauty. The beauty of her body is not the essence of her soul and she is a flapper, a 'susciety gurl' 'a sort of bogus aristocrat', irresponsible and careless whose only wish is to remain beautiful and young as long as possible. Her dazzling beauty attracts Anthony and her attitude towads life with no responsibility bring them together. She fully agrees with Anthony's idea of being 'gracefully lazy'. So when Anthony states – "I Do nothing, for there's nothing I can do that's worth doing . . . I don't understand why people think that every young mad ought to go down-town and work ten hours a day for the best twenty years of his life at dull, unimaginative work, certainly not altruistic work",[5] Gloria supports this statement and replies – "I don't mind if they don't do anything. I don't see why they should; in fact it always astonishes me when anybody does anything."[6]

Anthony qualifies her criterion to be 'graceful and companionable' and he allows his serenity to be destroyed by her pretentious self. Illusion of dream to be loved by this young beauty makes the romantic aesthete ignore the self-criticism offered by Gloria that she has got a streak of cheapness and likes things of 'bright colours' and 'gaudy vulgarity'. Rather 'the sheath that held her soul' bewildered him. Her alluring beauty destroyed Anthony's serenity and disturbed his aloofness from the world. His profound love for her makes him blind to the fact that she was beautiful, but she was without mercy. He cannot tolerate her intimacy with anyone else and hates to accept Bloeckman as his rival. Despite his limited income, his desire to be irresponsible and independent, he builds hope desperately and tenacioulsy out of the stuff of his dream wishing this hope to be 'the brawn and sinew to this self-respect' and eagerly awaits 'the radiant hour' to win the 'golden girl' – the mortal incarnation of damnation. He passes restless days, 'halycon days like boats drifting along slow-moving rivers' and is swept by the fervour of romance "not knowing that they were but following in the footsteps of dusty generations but comprehending dimly that if truth is the end of life happiness is a mode of it, to be cherished in its brief and tremulous moment".[7]

'The radiant hour' comes with 'the loveliness of the June' yielding 'a languorous and pleasant content' that settles like a weight upon him 'bringing responsibility and possession for Anthony. But for Gloria marriage is simply a means to satisfy her vanity. "Marriage was created not to be background but to need one. Mine is going to be outstanding. It can't, shan't be the setting – its going to be the performance, the live, lovely glamorous performance, and the world shall be the scenery."[8]

Gloria prefers to remain a permanent mistress and not be a 'wife'. Very soon Anthony discovers that "he was living with a girl of tremendous nervous tension and of the most high-handed selfishness", "with neither personal magnetism nor a loyal heart".[9] Her 'hard selfishness' naturally demands Anthony to be 'steadier' and 'more industrious' as his grandfather also had wanted him to be. She is irreconcilable and if she wants anything she must have it and she cannot be bothered resisting things she wants. In their wild drive for happiness they move from place to place carrying a host of new dreams. Not the tie of love but the expectation of inheritance keeps them together and they squander time and money to stimulate their tired nerves through several highballs and wild parties. Idleness breeds boredom that haunts them in an 'eternal monotone' – "What then, Oh, what'll we do then?"[10].

Anthony finds no incentive from "Gloria the idler, caresser of her own dreams extracting poignancy from the memorable things of life and youth."[11] Moreover, "Gloria had lulled Anthony's mind to sleep. She, who seemed of all women the wisest and the finest, hung like a beautiful curtain across his doorways shutting out the light of sun."[12] Anthony feels that if he had not met her he would have done something. Her charm to make leisure so subtly attractive combines with Anthony's lack of toughness and zeal to work. He broods from sheer inactivity and the receding hope to belong to the envied group of 'efficient people of leisure'. He tries in vain to finish his proposed history of the Middle Ages and fails to earn anything by writing commercial short stories as suggested by his successful friend Richard Caramel. Gloria wishes to join movies to break the monotony as well as to publicize her glamour.

Anthony objects to this, fearing that she may be lost in that dazzling world of various temptations. So they allow themselves to be swept by their reckless and extravagant way of life and invite their ruin unconsciously. Anthony compromises his serenity and succumbs to the whims of Gloria who wants nothing, "except to be young and beautiful, to be gay and happy, and to have money and love".[13] Being restless, Anthony tries to live on mere 'excitement' and 'fun' and every dose of high-ball adds to his growing misery and wrecks him slowly.

The situation becomes worse with the sudden visit of Adam Patch, the prohibitionist and the staunch Victorian, at the climax of a drunken party in Anthony's house. The old millionaire feels utterly shocked at this extravagant and irregular aspect of Anthony's life and immediately he quits the place. His decision to disinherit Anthony smashes the castle of imagination of Anthony and Gloria. Anthony's earlier speculations on future happiness and love – "how they were to travel from summer land to summer land, returning eventually to a gorgeous estate and possible idyllic children, then entering diplomacy or politics, accomplish for a white, beautiful and important things, until finally as a white-haired (beautifully, silkily, white-haired) couple they were to loll about in serene glory, worshipped by the bourgeoisie of the land . . ." are crashed with the loss of legacy.[14] Their increasingly irregular and increasingly dissipated life becomes loveless and cheerless. The broken lute cannot play the happy tune to make them forget and go beyond the world of reality they live in. "They were like two goldfish in a bowl from which all the water had been drawn; they could not even swim across to each other."[15]

Anthony simply indulges in sad reminiscences how both of them one summer morning had started their journey in search of happiness from New York, "New York was home – the city of luxury and mystery, of preposterous hopes and exotic dreams."[16] That quest for happiness itself seems to have been more satisfying than anything he expected for evermore. Now for him – "There was no rest, no quiet. He had been futile in longing to drift and dream".[17]

Fitzgerald makes his character suffer the rule of destiny and like a preacher seems to sermonize that " . . . no one dreamed, without his dreams becoming fantastic nightmares of indecision and regret."[18] 'The sense of waste' always dormant in Anthony oppresses him periodically and at certain moments he realizes that – "After a fashion, we *have* had our good time, raised the devil, and we're in the state of paying for it."[19]

The days of moroseness become unbearable and to try to win back their lost fortune they file a suit, the progress of which compel them to spend heavily on it which makes them overburdened. External pressure and internal tensions make them nervous and bored and they seek change. At this time war provides a diversion for Anthony. He welcomes it and gets enlisted simply to be away from the living present without any hope and joy in it. In reality, he wishes to be away, for the time being, from Gloria whose beauty fails to be a source of love and inspiration. Both of them look forward to a time when love, "springing like the phoenix from its own ashes should be born again in its mysterious and unfathomable haunts".[20]

Life in military barracks is certainly a change for Anthony, but the hard routine and strict discipline contained in it irritates him. While stationed in a Southern military camp as "an inevitable result of his increasing carelessness about himself" he gets involved in a sordid love affair with Dorothy Raycroft. His need for excitement and stimulus from without draws him towards Dorothy. "The girl promised rest; the hours in her company each evening alleviated the morbid and inevitably futile poundings of his imagination. He had become a coward in earnest – completely the slave of a hundred disordered and prowling thoughts which were released by the collapse of the authentic devotion of Gloria that had been the chief jailor of his insufficiency."[21]

Anthony tries to refresh his wounded spirit through this new love affair but he has to pay the price for his inability to make definite judgements. His passion for Dorothy makes him desperate to leave the camp at unsceheduled hours and break the military rules. Once he is caught and punished and stripped of his rank. He loses his respectability and suffers from melancholia again. He realizes at times how desire cheats and speaks of it to Dorothy – "It's like a sunbeam skipping here and there about a room. It stops and gilds some inconsequential object and we poor fools try to grasp it – but when we do the sunbeam moves on to something else, and you've got the inconsequential part, but the glitter that made you want it is gone . . . "[22] It exactly happens so in his case. Now the glitter of love for Dorothy is gone and in sheer hopelessness he feels anxious to get relieved from her. Armistice saves him from Dorothy and he comes back to New York.

Gloria, in the meantime, recognizing the failure of their love falls back on her old dream of beauty and youth. During Anthony's absence flirting becomes a pastime for her and she makes a fresh attempt to go into the movies for preserving the illusion of her beauty in celluloid – "She wanted to exist only as a conscious flower prolonging and preserving itself."[23] 'The old lure of screen' only reminds her bitterly that she is ageing and it makes the world melt before her eyes. This existence without hope, without happiness seems to be more oppressive and painful than death itself. Being unable to come to terms with reality she indulges in wishful thinking to revert to her virginal and colourful past'.

In the hands of time and reality both Anthony and Gloria become "like players who had lost their costumes, lacking the pride to continue on the note of tragedy" – and they take resort to the deceptive relief of drinking with the hope to recreate the lost atmosphere of dreamy sentimentalism and aestheticism. "There was a kindliness about intoxication – there is that indescribable gloss and glamour it gave, like the memories of ephemeral and faded evenings. . . . The fruit of youth or of the grape, the transitory magic of the brief passage from darkness to darkness – the old illusion that truth and beauty were in some way entwined."[24]

Bitterly Anthony realizes that nothing grows 'stale so soon as pleasure' and reproaches himself for indulging so long in the tropisms of pleasure. But it is too late now. His shattered nerves and lack of balance of mind bring him to the degrading point of unnecessary quarrelling and even fighting with Mr. Bloeckman. All these incidents reveal the decay of his inner self. Arrival of Dorothy in his New York apartment at this juncture of deterioration completely disintegrates him and leaves him paralysed. Ironically enough the moment of spiritual disinheritance is coincided with the regain of financial stability. At least he wins the legacy of thirty million dollars at the cost of mental poise and sanity indicating the hollowness of his victory. "Sailing off to Europe at novels end", as Joseph N. Riddel comments, "Anthony is trapped in the ironic isolation of his wealth and sysmbolically within his demented ego."[25]

No more he is Anthony of the past, very clean in appearance and in reality, but ruined to pieces caused by the hardships and insufferable tribulations for the mistakes of his youth. His craving for romance has exposed him to ruthless misery. Sparkling Gloria too seems "sort of dyed and *unclean*".[26]

Fitzgerald tries to justify Anthony in the line of Menckenian concept of hero who 'resists and fails' rather than yields and wins. So he adds in the conclusion –

> Anthony Patch, sitting near the rail and looking out at the sea, was not thinking of his money, for he had seldom in his life been really preoccupied with material vain glory, ... No – he was concerned with a series of reminiscences, much as a general might look back upon a successful campaign and analyse his victories. He was thinking of the hardships, the insufferable tribulations he had gone thorugh. They had tried to penalize him for him for the mistakes of his youth. He had been exposed to ruthless misery, his very craving for romance had been punished, his friends had

> deserted him – even Gloria had turned against him. He had been alone, alone – facing it all.[27]

Fitzgerald is troubled to raise the fallen image of his hero. He tries his best to defend the values and struggle of Anthony, who is really a problem child for him. Through the failure of his nerve and imagination Firzgerald depicts the decay of the romantic dream of self and enacts the death of possibility. Life of Anthony Patch indicates the gap between the world of his expectaion and the world of reality which he lives in. His inability to adjust his romantic self with the materialistic society, makes him suffer and be ruined. He is cheated by his own desire. The seed of his destruction lay within his dream. The glitter of wealth promises him the sunny side of life and the lure of beauty promises him love and happiness. Anthony expects to have all, but he gets none. He wishes to enjoy a leisurely life, but it becomes a muddled life for him. True, in his life he is seldom preoccupied with 'material vainglory', yet 'wealth for Anthony", as some critics think, is a means of escaping horror. Wealth and wealth only can keep him aloof from the air of struggle, of greedy amibition and hope of the middle class. He believes that to maintain aristocracy one needs a 'favourable environment' free from 'the warpings of ignorance and necessity', for developing cetain basic traits of it like 'courage, honour and beauty'.[28]

But ultimately this wealth, rather the dream of wealth distintegrates his soul and destroys his serenity which he adored most. Along with this instrument of evil Fitzgerald deals with the other deadlier agent of destruction, that is love of beauty, the beauty of Gloria. This 'la belle dame sans merci' is no less responsible for making Anthony invalid. It has been already discussed how she 'lulled him to sleep' and fuelling the inherent inertia of Anthony made leisure so subtly attractive for him. Anthony is possessed by her merciless beauty and selfish love and can never break the spell of it. All the distress he has undergone and the sorrow and the pain he experiences is rooted in this love of beauty – the beauty of woman.

Through Anthony's decay Fitzgerald reveals another important feature of the time – the reckless life of the youth without any regard for the past. Anthony's disaffection with the past makes him an easy prey to the zeitgeist. He is caught in the prevalent life of excess – both in manners and in morals. The youth in the post-war world specially finds no enduring resources to keep him in the right path of life. His ideas and ideals are shattered. He tries to sink his conscience in wild parties full of drinks and superficial gaiety, unknowingly hastening his own damnation. The lines of a song sung by Maury Noble in Anthony's apartment give us the picture of drunkenness and its inevitable results:

The – Pan-ic – has – come – over us,

So ha – a – as – the moral decline;[29]

These lines hint at the spiritual decay and the utter damnation of Anthony and Gloria too. They live in the 'sterile cocoon' of their irresponsible world and drift in pointlessness representing the dissolution of the age. Their embarkation for another world signify the new pursuit of happiness which they are refused here even at the cost of sanity and youth. So in the conclusion the author makes Anthony say – "I showed them. . . . It was a hard fight but I didn't give up and I came through!."

The story of Anthony and Gloria wrecking on the shoals of dissipation serves as a moral parable of Fitzgerald's moral earnestness. His craving for 'interior security' made him give due emphasis on moral integrity of the characters. The strong sense of morality of his upbringing could always be felt beneath the surface of his concern for the life of glamour and success. In a letter to his daughter he worte in 1939 – ". . . I guess I am too much a moralist at heart, and really want to preach at people in some acceptable form, rather than to entertain."[31] The characteristic division in his nature – the romantic exuberance and the moralistic sternness always worked together in him and marked all his writings. The dreamer and '*a spoiled priest*' – as he called himself in the

General Plan' for *Tender is the Night* – existed side by side in him and enabled him to sudy life in its true significance. He participated in life, full of enthusiams and excitement as a leading actor on the stage, yet at the same time judge it perfectly as a detached and cool observer sitting in the audience. All his works faeture this 'double vision' of him.

The Beautiful and Damned, even though less successful and less impressive than his mature writings like *The Great Gatsby* and others, yet it bears that stamp of characteristic distinction of Fitzgerald. He successfully develops the story as a moralizing tract against self-indulgence. The strain of self-indulgence spoils Anthony and causes his self-destruction. Unlike Amory Blaine Anthony fails to realize that *work is dignity*'. Not that he had any moral compunctions against work but in his idle imagination he wanted to be a 'gracefully lazy' American, keeping far above the 'air of struggle' and refused 'to give in, to submit to mediocrity, to go to work'. In Gloria he found his suitable partner who sought like him the life of pleasure only. Both of them tried to live in the world of romance and thrill as Fitzgerald and Zelda actually spent their married life in the early twenties like a 'fairy-story hero and heroine'.[32]

The life of Anthony and Gloria at this stage comes closer to the life of Fitzgeralds. It was for them a time "when the fulfilled future and the wasteful past were mingled in a single gorgeous moment – when life was literally a dream".[33] Anthony and Gloria took it for granted that their life would have a smooth sailing on love undisturbed by the pettiness of this mundane world. So they allowed themselves carelessly to be drifted in the world of pleasure expecting life to be a continuous show of 'blowing bubbles'. Gloria in her maiden days wrote in her diary about this sort of carefree life and make-believe happiness – "Blowing bubbles – that's what we're doing, Anthony and me. And we blew such beautiful ones to-day, and they'll exlpode and then we'll blow more and more. I guess – bubbles just as big and just as beautiful, until all the soap and water is used up."[34]

Initially life seemed to be a continuous party – "a gathering of persons who have a 'good time' only when highly stimulated by strong waters."[35] Zelda reflects on this spirit later in her *Save Me The Waltz*.

"We're having some people", everybody said to everybody else, "and we want you to join us," and they said, "we'll trelephone". All over New York people telephoned. They telephoned from one hotel to another, to people on their parties that they couldn't get there – that they were engaged. It was always tea-time or late at night. . . . Up they went humming the New Testament and our Country's Constitution riding the tide like triumphant islanders on a surf board. Nobody knew the words to "The Star – spangled Banner".[36]

The bubbling excitement of Gloria and Anthony was very soon over. Their love for pleasure could not sustain their life for long and they began to feel lonely and bored. The beautiful idyll of intense romance passed quickly with the current of time and wild ecstatic parties could no more charm them. They simply served as an escape from loneliness. The experience of Anthony and Gloria at this time reflects the same strain of painful boredom and conflict suffered by the Fitzgerald. As Fitzgerald says:

> The idyl passed, bearing with it its extortion of youth. . . . But knowing they had had the best of love, they clung to what remained. Love lingered – by way of long conversations at night into those stark hours when the mind thins and sharpens and the borrowings from dreams become the stuff of all life, by way of deep and intimate kindnesses they developed toward each other, by way of their laughing at the same absurdities and thinking the same things noble and the same things sad.[37]

Fitzgerald's puritan conscience and moral insight did not fail to mark the catastrophe in the midst of all bewilderment of Anthony and Gloria. In his portrait of 'The Beautiful' he imagined of what was to come out of their own lives and the doom of Anthony and Gloria projected his belief "that life is too strong and remorseless for the sons of men".[38] So, self-indulgent Anthony and Gloria, who tried to evade reality and wanted to live in golden moments only became stripped of their self-integrity and were damned forever. Thus *The Beautiful and Damned*, as Perosa sums up, "is a parable on the deceptiveness of dreams, on the impossibility of evading reality through illusion, and on the painful destructiveness of time."[39]

Mizener while evaluating the novel *The Beautiful and Damned* as one having a central purpose and meaning, and revealing Fitzgerald's "acute sense of disaster and his ability to realize the minutiae of humiliation and suffering",[40] points out Fitzgerald's failure to create Anthony convincingly 'sensitive and intelligent' and to provide adequate cause for his suffering.[41] Therefore, Anthony, according to him is not more sinned against than sinning. It is true, Fitzgerald was in great difficulty to justify the suffering of such a character with incurable lethargy and disdain for labour. He cannot fit Anthony in the line of his romantic heroes with their incorruptible dream and indomitable will to make life a success. Their suffering is justified in context of their noble cause and their struggle against the hostile society with its brutal power of wealth and therefore, their defeat is tragic. Anthony, on the other hand, "is tempted to cowardice by his imagination: he cannot blame others for his failures and fight them because of that old quality of understanding too well to blame – that quality which was the best of him and had worked swiftly and ceaselessly toward his ruin."[42] Consequently, Mizener thinks that Anthony's defeat is merely pathetic and not a tragic one.

But Fitzgerald never intended to endow Anthony with lofty character traits and tragic height; rather in the very beginning he made it clear that Anthony and Gloria represented 'Character in decay' and his purpose was to show how they wrecked on the shoals of dissipation." Accordingly, he portrayed Anthony with that taint of self-indulgence unwilling to accept a conventional career and at the same time lacking in more intellectual creative inspiration to do something. But that does not indicate that Anthony was utterly condemnable. He had his dream that "he would one day accomplish some quiet subtle thing that the elect would deem worthy and, passing on, would join the dimmer stars in a nebulous, indeterminate heaven half-way between death and immortality."[43] Fitzgerald started the story of Anthony as a "distinct and dynamic personality . . . a man who was aware that there could be no honour and yet had honour, who knew the sophistry of courage and yet was brave".[44] At the end of the story, the Anthony whom we see is not that same Anthony at the beginning.

Anthony Patch of the past was reduced to an empty shell whose spirit was totally dinsintegrated. He had been sufficiently penalized for the 'mistakes of his youth'. His great folly was his refusal to compromise with the actual world he lived in; and that made him undergo insufferable tribulations and experience the bitter realization that life is not all 'rosy and romantic' as it seemed to be. He had won in the suit of inheriting the legacy but was totally defeated in the pursuit of happiness. 'The Victor belongs to the spoils.' The sense of waste and 'touch of disaster' of which Fitzgerald wrote several years later can be felt in this early work too:

> With the end of the winter set in another pleasant pumped-dry period, and, while I took a little time off, a fresh picture of life in America began to form before my eyes. The uncertainties of 1919 were over — there seemed little doubt about what was going to happen — America was going on the greatest, gaudiest spree in history and there was going to be plenty to tell about it. The whole golden boom was in the air — its splendid generosities, its outrageous corruptions and the tortuous

> death struggle of the old America in prohibition. All the stories that came into my head had a touch of disaster in them – the lovely young creatures in my novels went to ruin, the diamond mountains of my short stories blew up, my millionaires were as beautiful and damned as Thomas Hardy's peasants. In life these things hadn't happened yet, but I was pretty sure living wasn't reckless, careless business these people thought – this generation just younger than me.[45]

Throughout the novel Fitzgerald harped on this tragic flaw in Anthony which debarred him from coming to grip with reality and pitilessly exposed him to disastrous consequences. But at the very end he defended the value of his struggle even though the struggle yielded to mere decadence. Fitzgerald showed that Anthony stuck to his ideal – "the rights and privileges of his own undemonstrated intellectual superiority" to the very point ot his loss of self-integrity. If we set Anthony's defeat against the so-called victory of Richard Caramel and Maury Noble – the other important characters of the story, then we would find that the success achieved by both of them at the cost of compromise of their 'selves' with the demands of the materialistic world, is less significant and impressive than the tragic failure of Anthony.

Richard Caramel, a successful writer compromised with his own standard and wrote inferior novels and commercial stories for the sake of money and popularity. 'Poor Dick', as Anthony used to call him was so blind that he could not know the great amount of sacrifice he had made for the cause of cheap popularity. Rather he boasted before Anthony who, too, once dreamt to be a writer, "My publisher, you know, have been advertising me as the Thackeray of America."[46] Anthony, of course, realized the full magnitude of Caramel's self-delusion. He knew that it had become the custom among young and clever reviewers to mention Richard Caramel with a smile of scorn. "His corpse was dragged obscenely through every literary supplement. He was accused of making a great fortune by writing trash for the movies. As the fashion in books shifted he was becoming almost a byword of contempt."[47]

Caramel's success was no real success. He gained financial security no doubt but lost his integrity as a writer. In that sense he is more damned than Anthony is. Fitzgerald himself had to trade his talent, waste his gift, and strain his resources for writng commercial stories to meet the demands of imperious Zelda, who like Gloria believed in her rights to have pretty things for preserving her beauty. So it seems quite natural on his part to justify Anthony for not submitting to the trivial necessaries of life. Caramel's success in that sense, makes him less important and rather undignified than Anthony, – a victim of lethargy and self-pity.

So also is the point of difference with Maury Noble. At the outset he is a self-ordained sceptic and remains highly cynical throughout the novel. Fitzgerald seems to suggest that Maury's pathetic cynicism makes him compromise with his humanistic ideals and he develops a contemptuous attitude towards his fellow men. Ultimately he becomes a ruthless materialist and even disdains to help his dissipated friend Anthony. He becomes totally devoid of thought or intellect and succumbs to a respectable middle-class marriage. "He was sorry for no one now – on Monday morning there would be his business, and later there would be a girl of another class whose whole life he was; these were the things nearest his heart. In the strangeness of the brightening day it seemed presumptuous that with this feeble, broken instrument of his mind he had ever tried to think."[48] This fact of compromise and inability to retain a fine creative mind proves his downfall more damnable than Anthony's.

Fitzgerald laid the story of Anthony and Gloria in his own time and made the characters face the challenge of time whether successful or not. He observed life and his society from a close angle and gave voice to his feelings and emotions in his stories. *The Beautiful and Damned* is no exception. It reveals his emotional identification with his characters which speak of his sympathy for them and at the same time it tries to give an objective development of his characters according to a rigorous thematic principle. In handling Anthony he had to do the hard task of detaching himself to stand aside and unfold his character in all its complexities. He shared some of the illusions of his protagonist and had sympathy for his failure. As a result he felt like justifying the greatness of his struggle. In *The Beautiful and Damned* Fitzgerald had "to expose and denounce two characters who appealed to him, or to justify their beauty in spite of their damnation."[49]

As regards his moralistic attitude and theme of individual failure are concerned, Fitzgerald owed to H. L. Mencken for his principles of new schools of writing which he called 'ironical – pessimistic'. Mencken maintained that the interest of a 'superior fiction' lay in the representation of the conflict 'between a salient individual and the harsh and meaningless fiats of destiny', in the struggle of a hero who is not 'one who yields and wins, but one who resists and fails.' The theme of the great bulk of superior fiction, he stated, is 'character in decay'.[50] Fitzgerald followed this literary principle as stated by Mencken and accordingly drew the 'character in decay' – Anthony and Gloria – and showed their defeat.

Critics are of opinion that his Anthony, in point of his deterioration, comes in the line of Hurstwood (*Sister Carrie*) and Vandover (*Vandover and the Brute*) and they find many things in common with the writings of Theodore Dreiser and Frank Norris – the naturalistic writers dealing with the same theme of individual failure.

Dreiser's *Sister Carrie* presents Hurstwood as a 'pilgrim adream', whose dream too, like Anthony's becomes a lethargy and then a nightmare. He too is without a regular job and wastes away his life in a sordid room and in the company of shabbier friends, drifts along the empty streets, hopelessly drinking and suffering from the inner dejection and helplessness. But in his case the economic and social factors are more responsible for his ruin though he, too, has a tragic flaw – his hamartia. His destiny is more tragic caused by the ruthless laws of his business world; the deep-rooted social prejudices of middle class philistinism; and finally desertion of Carrie.

Similarly, parallel influence of Frank Norris may be felt in Fitzgerald's attempt of 'moralizing tract against self-indulgence'. In its thematic design *The Beautiful and Damned* shows much affinity with that of Norris' *Vandover and the Brute*. Vandover's dissipation does nort result from his impotent attempts to act in opposition to a determined fate; rather his destruction results from his own apathy. Like Anthony he suffers from a destructive self-indulgence. He is represented as a promising artist preoccupied with idle-pleasures wasting his talent. Vandover is equally self-indulgent and loves sensuous pleasures. He hates to be bored and worried and wishes to have a good time.

Vandover acts not to achieve success as his father intended but to avoid the displeasing situations in life in which he has been dragged into. For his irresponsibility Ida Wade commits suicide which touches him very little and proves him incapable of true love. After his father's death a new life begins for Vandover, a life of luxury and aimlessness which he finds charming. He has no duties, no cares, no responsibilities. Rapidly his 'pliable character' lacking both the desire and necessary to keep him at work moves toward deterioration. He refuses to act even when he is threatened with financial disaster and reaches a state of absolute indifference. He has mere passive existence – with no ambitions, no cares, no hopes, no regrets. Vandover with his lethargic indifferences is ultimately doomed in a society – the society which insists on human effort and action to get true happiness in life..

These discussions may help us to know Fitzgerald's indebtedness to his contemporaries and show their influence on him. But to judge his merit and originality we may state that Fitzgerald derived the material of his stories from his own life. He used to dig himself up and reveal his own emotions and feelings through the created characters presented in the different situations of life. His brilliant gift of imagination empowered him to visualize the situation and experiences to which he projected his own self and contemplated the possibilities arising out of them. *The Beautiful and Damned* was such an attempt where he projected not only his own self but that too of his wife Zelda. Their own married life provided the material for certain situations and even conversations in the novel. He portrayed the contemporary reckless life and revealed its inevitable results to give a comprehensive view of life. His ambition to be a great writer invoked him to deal with the more serious aspects of life deep in the realm of stern morality as a contrary to the brilliant surface of irresponsible gaiety.

The Beautiful and Damned is not a futile attempt, as has often been assumed, to describe the glorified illusion of human dreams. Anthony and Gloria were victims of a romantic conception of the world. Their story is developed as a moral parable – the parable of the youthful dreams and illusions that gradually become a lethargy and then a nightmare ultimately leading to an inevitable ruin. Fitzgerald the romantic is in the role of a moralist too. Here he is concerned with exposing the inner meaning of life, not merely reproducing its brilliant surface. He is concerned with suffering and bitter aspects of experience, not with playful manifestations. He reveals the hidden flaw of failure and defeat of the 'beautiful' latent in their glamorous, and careless way of life. Anthony's problem is rooted in his disaffection with the past. He stands at the door of a new age with sensitivity and longing, but without direction or purpose. Anthony portrays the destruction of a 'personage' who, lacking Amory's creative energy of hope falls into the slough of despair. His incapacity for hope, his unwillingness to sacrifice himself to a dream, his intellectual disdain for labour and his refusal to compromise with reality result in inner and outer ruin. His artistic sense is dissipated for the purchase of an empty future.

The novel is divided into three books, each in turn divided into three chapters. Each book represents a distinct moment in the development of the story, while the chapters themselves mark the progressive unfolding of the parable. As in *This Side of Paradise*, here too, the action is based on the development of the characters, though the development is a negative one – a process of deterioration. There are frequent intrusions of the author himself to advocate "some recent ideas of his own and possibly of others". (*Letters*, p. 328) And though there is very little open discussion of philosophical or social problems, the novel serves as a vehicle for the exposition of a social problem.

The principle of inclusion or discursiveness is responsible for the excessive length of the book. The secondary episodes and characters are not always relevant to the main theme. The links between one episode and another are often casual, and sometimes presented as isolated facts which gives an impression of 'Confused fresco'. (Perosa, p. 49) Fitzgerald himself was aware of this fact and in a letter to John Peale Bishop he wrote: "I devoted so much more care myself to the *detail* of the book than I did to thinking out the *general* theme". (*Letters*, p. 353) Moreover, the old device of alternating parts of pure dialogue with proper narration is used without proper force and significance.

In this novel Fitzgerald seems to have lost his gift for 'writing naturally in sentences'. Here his sentences are long and twisted, elaborate and overloaded with images. The round-about expressions make the sentence heavy and deaden its fluency. The quality of his language is greatly compromised.

The Beautiful and Damned, however shows some development over its predecessor. With this novel Fitzgerald achieves, though in a limited way, a greater objectivity upon his materials, a detachment from his hero. He succeeds in having a mature ironic tone. He offers a determinist view of life and momentary flashes of self-knowledge in it anticipate the perfect dramatization of the self in its two existing aspects of ideal and practical being as revealed in *The Great Gatsby*. The novel takes Fitzgerald one step further towards maturity in artistic craftsmanship specially in his natural sense of the dramatic interplay between self and environment. Nevertheless, *The Beautiful and Damned* has its merits as a successful attempt to probe new fictional depths, and as such it can be regarded as a considerable achievement in the catalogue of Fitzgerald's fiction. Fitzgerald the conscientious artist tries to do the "duty of a sincere writer – to set down life as he sees it as gracefully as he knows how". (*Letters*, p. 141) We can conclude with the comment of H.L. Mencken who thought that in this book Fitzgerald "tried something much more difficult, and if the result is not a complete success, it is nevertheless near enough to success to be worthy of respect. There is fine observation in it, and much penetrating detail, and the writing is solid and sound. . . . "

There are ... signs in it of serious purpose and unquestionable skill. Even in its defects there is proof of hard striving. Fitzgerald ceases to be a *Wunderkind*, and begins to come into his maturity". (H.L. Mencken, "The Niagara of Novels", pp. 140-41)

References

1. Andrew Turnbull, *Letters of F. Scott Fitzgerald*, New York: Scribner's 1963, p. 145.
2. F. Scott Fitzgerald, *The Beautiful and Damned*, New York: Scribner's, 1950, pp. 11-12.
3. *Ibid.*, p. 18.
4. *Ibid.*, pp. 45-46.
5. *Ibid.*, p. 65.
6. *Ibid.*, p. 66.
7. *Ibid.*, p. 137.
8. *Ibid.*, p. 147.
9. *Ibid.*, p. 179.
10. *Ibid.*
11. *Ibid.*, p. 169.

12. *Ibid.*, p. 191.
13. *Ibid.*, p. 276.
14. *Ibid.*, p. 277.
15. *Ibid.*, p. 276.
16. *Ibid.*, p. 282.
17. *Ibid.*
18. *Ibid.*
19. *Ibid.*, p. 305.
20. *Ibid.*, p. 308.
21. *Ibid.*, p. 325.
22. *Ibid.*, p. 341.
23. *Ibid.*, p. 393.
24. *Ibid.*, p. 417.
25. Joseph N. Riddel, " The Jamesian Inheritance, and the Morality of Fiction", *Modern Fiction Studies,* V. II, 1965, p. 342.
26. *The Beautiful and Damned,* p. 448.
27. *Ibid.*, p. 449.
28. *Ibid.*, p. 407.
29. *Ibid.*, p. 238.
30. *Ibid.*, p. 449.
31. F. Scott Fitzgerald, *The Crack-Up,* New York: New Directions Paperbook, 1956, p. 305.
32. Authur Mizener,, *The Far Side of Paradise,* Boston, Houghton Mifflin Company, 1965, p. 27.
33. F. Scott Fitzgerald, "The Early Success", *The Crack-Up,* p. 9.
34. *The Beautiful and Damned,* p. 147.
35. Authur Mizener, *The Far Side of Paradise,* p. 124.
36. Zelda Fitzgerald, *Save Me The Waltz,* Carbondale and Edwardaville: Southern Illinois University Press, 1967, p. 48.
37. *The Beautiful and Damned,* p. 156.
38. Andrew Turnbull, *Letters of F. Scott Fitzgerald,* New York: Scribner's 1963, p. 462.

39. Sergio Perosa, *The Art of F. Scott Fitzgerald,* Ann Arbor, The University of Michigan Press, 1969, p. 41.
40. *The Far Side of Paradise*, pp. 154-55.
41. *Ibid.*, p. 155.
42. *Ibid.*
43. *The Beautiful and Damned,* p. 3.
44. *Ibid.*, p. 3.
45. "The Early Success", *The Crack-Up*, p. 87.
46. *The Beautiful and Damned*, p. 423.
47. *Ibid.*, pp. 421-22.
48. *Ibid.*, p. 260.
49. Sergio Perosa, *The Art of F. Scott Fitzgerald*, p. 46.
50. H.L. Mencken, *Prejudices: Second Series*, New York: 190, pp. 38-41.

8

The Great Gatsby
The Saga of an Innocent Abroad

As a conscientious artist F. S. Fitzgerald sought some quintessential national impulse underlying the surface gaiety of his generation. He immersed himself so much in the contemporary life of hedonistic pleasures that one may think that he completely lost his 'self' in that world. But however engrossed he might have been, he was never 'taken in' by that surface life. He possessed a rare gift of profound understanding and a sharp critical intelligence to look into the real nature of things. He lived in moments and could recreate those moments in tranquil imagination. So the experiences he revealed are not merely felt experiences of a particular moment but have a touch of permanence in them. They glow with the recreated feelings of an imaginative artist and cool observations of a moral critic. His romantic involvement with life yielded to ultimate realization of the bitter truth that in the brittle, moneyed world of America no dream of love or happiness can survive without the support of wealth.

Wealth for Americans seemed to act as 'fins and wings' to escape the shoddy reality and fulfil the promises of life. The American dream that essentially believed in the romantic possibilities of life became tainted with the lure of money. As Bewley remarks: "The American dream which had started innocently enough when there had been a vast unexploited continent to support the possibilities it seemed to promise, had become brutalized as the only means or realizing them had more and more centred in money with the passing of the frontier and the advent of the Gilded Age."[1] The writings of Scott Fitzgerald repeatedly emphasize this inseperable link between American dream and American wealth. They deal with the fact how the eternal hope of the older religion has become debased in the material promises of the continent.

While showing the significance of wealth in realizing the possibilities of life Fitzgerald pointed out how the pristine innocence of individual is corrupted by glamour of wealth. His basic ideas and attitude towards the tragic fate of a romantic self are deep-rooted in the national grain. In his third novel, *The Great Gatsby,* Fitzgerald with his historian's instinct succeeds to find out the motives and gauge the temper of a particular period; while with a moralist's vision he successfully evaluates too, the momentary experience in light of traditional beliefs and the lasting values of life. As he stated: "I feel I have an enormous power in me now, more than I've ever had. . . . So in my new novel I'm thrown directly on purely creative work – not trashy imaginings as in my stories but the sustained imagination of a sincere yet radiant world."[2] Later in 1934, Fitzgerald would remark that never had he tried to keep his artistic conscience so pure as during the time of composition of *The Great Gatsby*. In a letter to the Kalmans, Zelda also expressed a similar view on Fitzgerald's ceaseless effort to write this novel: "Scott has started a new novel and retired into strict seclusion and celibacy. He's horribly intent on it. . . ."[3] Fitzgerald himself believed this novel to be "something new, something extraordinary and beautiful and simple and intricately patterned."[4] His creative temperament acquired new insights into old ideas.

The theme of amassing wealth destroying the purity of love gets its finest expression in the story of Jay Gatsby. As Fitzgerald made it quite clear to one of his friends: " . . .the whole idea of Gatsby is the unfairness of a poor young man not being able to marry a girl with money. This theme comes up again and again because I lived it."[5] This same theme of youthful hope crushing against the tyranny of wealth and betrayal of love appear in sketchy form in some of his finest stories. Specially 'Winter Dreams' and 'The Sensible Thing' — these two stories present almost the similar idea as in *The Great Gatsby* — the longed — for wealth cannot bring back the lost moment of love and youth.

Young Dexter in 'Winter Dreams' who has risen from a caddy on the golf course to a successful industrialist only to win the love of irresponsible Judy, fails to stop the fleeting moment of beauty and love. And so he is left with a deep regret for youthful illusion shattered by reality. Like Judy's beauty his dream becomes a victim to the remorselessness of time. He mourns over the loss: "The Dream was gone. Something had been taken from him. . . . He wanted to care, and he could not care. For he had gone away and he could never go back any more. The gates were closed, the sun was gone down, and there was no beauty but the gray beauty of steel that withstands all time. Even the grief he could have borne was left behind in the country of illusion, of youth, of the richness of life, where his winter dreams had flourished."

"Long ago", he said, "long ago, there was something in me, but now that thing is gone. Now that thing is gone, that thing is gone. I cannot cry. I cannot care. That thing will come no more."[6]

In 'The Sensible Thing' George O'Kelly with his sudden wealth wins back the love of Jonquil who had left him earlier because he was poor. But this apparent victory of George is obtained at the cost of incurable loss of youthful emotion and freshness of feelings: " . . . he knew that that boy of fifteen months before had had something, a trust, a warmth that was gone forever. The sensible thing — they had done the sensible thing. He had traded his first youth for strength and carved success out of despair. But with his youth, life had carried away the freshness of his love."[7] Kelly expresses his sense of despair and loss — "April is over, April is over. There are all kinds of love in the world, but never the same love twice."[8]

The Great Gatsby expands these slender suggestions in fullest implication and with a definite consecration transforms Gatsby's dream into a universal tragedy. In this fiction Fitzgerald set the plot around an agonizing conflict of the moral and social order and enlarged its meaning on the symbolic level of legend and myth. He depicted the flowering and decay of Gatsby's personal dream as having a parallel significance in the national life of America and by implication, the humanity at large. In fact, Gatsby's experience is the experience of the unfallen innocent who shares the romantic vision of the early dreamers and meets the tragic destiny for his commitment to ideals. His story represents the utter impossibility of pursuing romantic dreams in an unromantic world. His quest for a lost past is the age-old search for a 'brave new world'.

In Gatsby's journey from Middle West to Long Island, Fitzgerald traces the character's evolution from Jimmy Gatz to Jay Gatsby. Within the brief span of the novel Fitzgerald dramatizes the events of a single summer and the facts preceding before them through a series of scenes and flashbacks. He introduces the characters through Nick Carraway who narrates the story in bits and pieces projecting the gradual development of the characters and shaping the moral vision of the author himself. James or Jimmy as his father calls him (Gatsby), a poor farm boy from North Dakota, aspires to rise and be great in the manner of Benjamin Franklin. He cannot accept his humble origin. He tries to repudiate his former identity by dissociating himself from his parents – the "shiftless and unsuccessful farm people". (p.99) In the words of Nick, "the truth was that Jay Gatsby of West Egg, Long Island, sprang from his Platonic conception of himself. He was a son of God – a phrase which, if it means anything, means just that – and he must be about His Father's business, the service of a vast, vulgar, and meretricious beauty". (p. 99) Indeed, Gatsby is shown later as a self-made man who in his yearning for 'meretricious beauty' sacrifices his life.

Initially James Gatz beats his way along the south shore of

Lake Superior as a clam-digger and a salmon-fisher. But his heart is always in a 'turbulent riot' with a constant yearning for 'future glory'. (pp.99-100) He is haunted by 'most grotesque and fantastic conceits': "A universe of ineffable gaudiness spun itself out in his brain. . . . Each night he added to the pattern of his fancies. . . . For a while these reveries provided as outlet for his imagination; they were a satisfactory hint of the unreality of reality, a promise that the rock of the world was founded securely on a fairy's wing." (p. 100)

World's "ferocious indifference to the drum of his destiny" makes him dismayed. (p. 100) He goes on searching for something to do and at such a moment of despair Dan Cody's yatcht anchors on Lake Superior. To Gatz's mind it seems to represent "all the beauty and glamour in the world". (pp. 100-01) Cody at the same time, finds in Gatsby a "quick and extravagantly ambitious" youth. (p. 101) He takes him in his yatch and along with *Tuolomee* James Gatz leaves for a new shore under the new name of Jay Gatsby.

Dan Cody who turns up as James Gatz's destiny, is a product of the Nevada silver fields whom much later in the novel Nick describes as "a gray, florid man with a hard, empty face – the pioneer debauchee, who during one phase of American life brought back to the Eastern seabord the savage violence of the frontier brothel and saloon". (p. 101) Gatsby stays with this man for five years till Cody's death and serves him in different capacities starting from steward to secretary. He learns a lesson from Cody's drunkenness and loose morals. Cody reposes more and more trust in Gatsby and leaves a legacy of twenty-five thousand dolllars. Gatsby of course, cannot enjoy the same as Ella Kaye, Cody's woman deprives him of it. Nick states the situation: "He was left with his singularly appropriate education; the vague contour of Jay Gatsby had filled out to the substantiality of a man". (p. 102)

With the advent of the First World War Gatsby leads an army officer's life in a training camp at Kentucky. Daisy Fay, a lovely southern girl enchants him as the first 'nice' girl that he has ever known. (p. 148) In his eyes Daisy appears to be extraordinary, "gleaming like silver, safe and proud above the hot struggles of the poor", "high in a white palace the king's daughter, the golden girl". (pp. 150, 120) In his youthful passionate idealistic, love for Daisy he forgets the fact, that he is "a penniless young man without a past, and at any moment the invisible cloak of his uniform might slip from him shoulders". (p. 149) His romantic nature makes him desperate and "under false pretences" deliberately he gives Daisy "a sense of security". (p. 149) But it is he himself who becomes trapped within his own desires and action while Daisy seems to be unaffected. In his great emotional commitment to Daisy his love becomes a sacred act like "the following of a grail". (p. 149) But Daisy on the contrary, is more concerned with her "artificial world . . . . redolent of orchids and pleasant, cheerful snobbery and orchestras . . ." (p. 151) In loving her, Gatsby loses "some idea of himself" that he can never recover and since then his life becomes "confused and disordered". (p. 111)

But to Gatsby himself the life appears to be a dream. The surrounding world seems to be trasfromed into something magical and enchanting partaking the glory of love. One autumn night – a cool moonlit night full of mysterious excitement – in his walk with Daisy Gatsby feels to be transported into another world into the land of stars. The magnitude of his romantic imagination and heroic vision of himself makes him see:

> . . . that the blocks of the sidewalks really formed a leader and mounted to a secret place above the trees – he could climb to it, if he climbed alone, and once there he could suck on the pap of life, gulp down the incomparable milk of wonder.
>
> His heart beat faster and faster as Daisy's white face came up to his own. He knew that when he kissed this girl, and forever wed his unutterable visions to her perishable

> breath, his mind would never romp again like the mind of God. So he waited, listening for a moment longer to the tuning-fork that had been struck upon a star. Then he kissed her. At his lips' touch she bolssomed for him like a flower and the incarnation was complete.[9]

But in actuality Daisy never blooms like a flower for Gatsby, rather she remains as a "human orchid of woman". (p. 106) Her kisses are tinged with frigidity. After playing with Gatsby's emotions for a while, she vanishes into her "rich house, into her rich, full life, leaving Gatsby — nothing". (p. 149)

Sometime after Gatsby goes abroad on his commision, Daisy starts keeping "half a dozen dates a day with half a dozen man". (p. 151) Wasting no time in brooding over Gatsby's love she decides to marry a new acquaintance Tom Buchanan who has a bulkiness about his person and his position". (p. 151) Nick's comment brings out the enormous power and the aggressive and supercilious manner of Tom when he remarks that : "it was a body capable of enormous leverage — a cruel body". (p. 7) Daisy too, realizes this truth, though much later, in their conjugal life that in marrying Tom she has married "a brute of a man,. a great, big hulking physical specimen. . ." (p. 12) Indeed, throughout the novel the brutal power of Tom dominates over all those, specially who are close to them – like Daisy and Myrtle – his wife and his mistress.

Returning from abroad Gatsby revisits Louisville. Though Daisy is no more there, still her memory seems to make the place pervading with a "melancholy beauty". (p. 153) In a flashback one can see Gatsby stretching out his hand desperately" as if to snatch only a wisp of air, to save a fragment of the spot that had made lively for him". (p. 153) Gatsby cannot accept the bare truth that he has lost Daisy for ever. He is still naive enough to believe that he can regain Daisy and their youthful ecstasy merely through wealth. To Carraway's warning that "You can't repeat the past"

Gatsby replies "Why of course you can". (p. 111) He takes riches as the means of achieving the golden vision of love and life. To make this dream come true he resorts to dubious means and builds a fortune on fraud and violence. He comes in contact with Meyer Wolfsheim, a gambler, "the man who fixed the World's Series back in 1919". (p. 74) Like Dan Cody, Wolfsheim discovers in Gatsby "a fine-appearing gentlemanly young man", whom hé can utilize in his underground business. So he raises him up to a big bootlegger, "out of nothing, right out of gutter", from the state of "a young major just out of the army and covered over with medals, . . . wearing his uniform because so hard up that he cannot buy some regular clothes and has to go without food for days together. (p. 172)

In his partnership with Meyer Wolfsheim, an ill reputed man, Gatsby acquires a sudden wealth; but his wealth is tainted no doubt. In trying to be faithful to his love and thus keeping true to his inner self he becomes oblivious of the 'foul dust' that float in "the wake of his dreams". (p. 2)

After five years when Nick Carraway happens to be Gatsby's neighbour, he finds Gatsby in a changed status possessing a fantastic mansion, "a factual imitation of some Hotel de Ville in Normandy, with a tower on one side, spanking a new under a thin beard of raw ivy, and a marble swimming pool, and more than forty acres of lawn and garden". (p. 5) At every week-end Gatsby's 'blue garden' becomes filled with men and girls "like moths among the whisperings and the champagne and the stars". (p. 39) But what attracts Nick more is something 'gorgeous' about Gatsby glowing in his "heightened sensitivity to the promises of life" and "an extraordinary gift for hope", "a romantic readiness" for life. (p.2) Nick feels amazed at Gatsby's silent watch for "a single green light, minute and far away, that might have been the end of a dock". (p. 32)

At the opposite end of the bay live Tom and Daisy in the fashionable East Egg. This geographical opposition brings out the social and moral contrast of the characters. Gatsby's unspoiled tender love has to face an opposition on the 'hard malice' of Buchanans. Nick at his first visit to Daisy's house becomes aware of the sharp difference between the Buchanan's way of living and the manners of the West. Their shallow sophistication makes him feel 'uncivilized'. (p.13) He feels uneasy in discovering Tom's adultery, Daisy's "basic insincerity". (p.18) As Nick is "slow-thinking and full of interior rules" and regards honesty to be one of the cardinal virtues – he feels disgusted with the artificial world of the Buchanans. Even Daisy's friend, Jordan Baker, the golf-champion is "incurably dishonest". (p.58) Nick at first feels attracted to her no doubt. But he cannot accept her because she lacks in honesty. In comparison to the insensitiveness of this 'rotten crowd'. the incorruptible dream of Jay Gatsby proves to be more worthy in Nick's eyes. (pp. 154-55)

But Gatsby as shown against the background of elaborate parties appears to others as a mysterious figure. The unknown, uninvited guests sharing in the pomposity of those parties gossip on his shady past and speculate over the secrets of his fabulous wealth. They believe him to be a gangster, a spy and even a murderer. Thus Gatsby's 'notoriety' increases, being spread about by the hundreds who have accepted his hospitality and so become "authorities upon his past". (p.98) Tom Buchanan is one of such guests who thinks Gatsby's respectability is no better than one of those 'newly rich people' who are just big bootleggers.

Daisy too fails to understand Gatsby's 'unwavering devotion' and is simply apalled by the splendour of Gatsby's wealth. In Gatsby's love she finds a relief from her boring life with nothing to do. In her conversation with Jordan Baker she shows her boredom and emptiness of feelings: "What'll we plan . . . what do people Plan"? (p.12) or again "What'll we do with ourselves this afternoon . . . and the day after that, and the next thrity years?" (p.118) Daisy, the product of leisure and wealth always watches for 'the longest day' in her idle imagination. She becomes impatient and feels disgusted and annoyed with philandering Tom. Gatsby's re-appearance on the scene makes her feel nostalgic about the youthful romances of her maidenhood. At Nick's invitation she gets a chance to meet Gatsby alone and finds an opportunity to have a change. Thereafter Daisy starts visiting Gatsby quite often – in the afternoon. And the whole 'caravansary' going on in Gatsby's place falls in like a 'card house' at the disapproval in Daisy's eyes. (p.114)

Gatsby is fooled again. His simplicity of faith and capacity for hope makes him believe that Daisy has never cared for Tom. He expresses his blithe confidence and a deep sense of anguish at the moment when Tom tries to expose and humiliate him before all in the Plaza suite: "She's never loved you. She loves me ......She only married you because I was poor and she was tired of waiting for me. It was a terrible mistake, but in her heart she never loved any one except me". (p. 131) But it is not Daisy rather Gatsby himself who commits the terrible mistake and connot know when the right moment to fulfil his love has become lost into the vast obscurity.

The intensity of Gatsby's dream blurs his vision. So he is unable to detect revulsion on Daisy's face when he asks her to leave Tom. In his illusion to win back the past and return to a 'certain starting place' he clutches at some 'last hope' and waits for Daisy's approval. (p. 148) But as the story unfolds, Daisy's emptiness has curdled into the "viciousness of a monstrous moral indifference".[10] Her behaviour suggests the callous ennui, the deathly hollowness of the 'golden girl'. The "exhilarating ripple of her voice" does not echo a 'deathless song' but echoes the jingle of money. She is not what she looks but what Gatsby sees in her, Indeed, in loving Daisy Gatsby has "thrown himself into it with a creative passion adding to it all the time, decking it out with every bright feather that drifted his way". (p.97)

But Daisy in her turn, refuses Gatsby's avowed love and behaves with a criminal amorality. When Gatsby chivalrously plans to shoulder the blame for Daisy's careless driving causing

Myrtle's death, she takes the opprtunity and carefully hides her own fault. Even after taking her home, Gatsby waits outside her window and keeps a sacred vigil still with the hope, that Daisy may need his protection. On the other hand, Daisy and Tom conspire together so that they can escape the consequences of the accident. Gatsby ramins totally unaware of the fact till the end and as the owner of 'the death car' meets his tragic end in being the target of Wilson, Myrtle's husband. His innocent dream is thus defeated by the 'hard malice' of the Buchanans. (p.148) Tom and Daisy, as members of "a rather distinguished secret society" ideally suit each other and become accomplices in making the 'holocaust complete' with Wilson's suicide.

Not only Gatsby, but also Wilson and Myrtle fall victims to the carelessness and arrogance of wealth represented by the so-called aristocracy of Tom and Daisy. Tom's hypocrisy and vulgar sensuality cheat the Wilsons – the members of the lower middle class. The splendour of Tom's wealth and his deceitful nature befool them. Tom exploits their poverty and stupidity. Myrtle, the fleshy sensuous woman, has a wild dream to own Tom. She tries to escape from her dreary life into the world of glamour through the false assurance given by Tom. Accordingly she tries to be lady like; buys a dog: dresses herself in tawdry finery; and gives parties in 'her' apartment. But when she tries to assert herself Tom breaks her nose. Tom simply amuses himself in her company; but he has no real intention to divorce Daisy as Myrtle expects him to do so. Myrtle's 'tremendous vitality' is ultimately crushed violently by Daisy only, equally heartless and careless like her husband. (p. 138)

The 'anaemic', 'spiritless', 'ghostly', 'ashen' figure of Wilson is a pathetic figure. His life is as miserable as the unprosperous garage that he has in the vicinity of the ash heaps. His economic condition compels him to seek some favour from ruthless Tom. He wishes to get away from this place and start a new life with Myrtle in the West. He is aware of tbe fact that Myrtle has "some sort of life apart from him in another world". (p.124) But "he's so dumb he doesn't know he's alive". (p.26) But Myrtle's violent death makes him hysteric and violent. In that confused state of mind Tom's malicious intention easily misdirects him to kill Gatsby as well as himself. The poor creature can never know that it is Tom only who under the guise of a well-wisher has been his betrayer both in love and in revenge.

So Nick's comment about Buchanan is quite justified:

> They were careless people, Tom and Daisy – they smashed up things and creatures and then retreated back into their money or their vast carelessness, or whatever it was that kept them together, and let other people clean up the mess they had made. . . (p.181)

Central to the novel's effect is the picture of this 'mess' as symbolized through 'Valley of ashes' depicting a sense of waste, desolation and futility. The atmosphere, the characterization and the events in the novel speak of the moral horror and disillusion represented by this abominable place, "halfway between West Egg and New York". (p.23) Nick pictures this desolate area of land – the valley of ashes as:

> a fanatastic farm where ashes grow like wheat into ridges and hills and grotesque gardens; where ashes take the forms of houses and chimneys and rising smoke and, finally, with a transcendent effort, of ash-gray men who move dimly and already crumbling through the powdery air. Occasionally a line of gray cars crawls along an invisible track, gives out a ghastly creak, and comes to rest, and immediately the ash-gray men swarm up with leaden spades and stir up an impenetrable cloud, which screens their obscure operations from your sight. (p. 23)

This 'valley of ashes' is like Eliot's wasteland where spiritless men become indistinguishable from the spiritless landscape. It symbolizes the non-human chaos, the broken images of undisciplined fragmentation of modern life. The imagery of disorder is distinctly revealed through the staring eyes of Dr. T.J. Eckleburg in the faded advertisement that overlooks the gray land. Dominating the land of dust and endless drift are the eyes of Eckleburg on an abandoned billboard. Eckleburg is a grotesque god of advertising with retinas one yard high which "look out of no face, but, instead from a pair of enormous yellow spectacles which pass over a non-existent nose". (p.23) In the gray land the advertised spectacles put there by an oculist 'to fatten his practice' provide the only colour – the garishness of the sign is accented by the yellow colour, unsuited to genuine spectacles. Eckleburg's billboard has been abandoned, and the emptiness of its promise is evident. The oculist who erected the eyes of Eckleburg "sank down himself into eternal blindness, or forgot them and moved away". (p.23)

This grotesque image of Doctor T.J. Eckleburg reappearing throughtout the story, eventually becomes a persistent symbol of moral chaos. A feeling of hopelessness pervades the whole atmosphere which may well strengthen one's conviction that contemporary society in its present stage is ruled by a complex of forces destructive of basic human values and subversive of man's vision of the good life.

The final tragedy of the novel reinstates this truth in Gatsby's death. Gatsby's sincere belief in the promises of life keeps him ignorant of the frauds of society, the brutal forces that victimize him. So at last he has to pay "a high price for living too long with a single dream". (p.162)

After Gatsby's death Nick Carraway withdraws from the East – the East which excited him most and made him leave the Middle West since it seemed like "the ragged edge of the universe". (p.3) Now this East for Nick has simply " a quality of distortion". (p.177) And he expresses his disillusionment: "the East was haunted for me . . . distorted beyond my eyes' power of correction. So when the blue smoke of brittle leaves was in the air and the wind blew the wet laundry stiff on the line I decided to come back home". (p.178)

Nick comes back home – the Carraway house in a city in the Middle West. In comparison to East, Middle West now seems to him as "the thrilling returning trains" of his youth. (p.177) The East represented by Tom and Daisy, Jordan and others falls short of Nick's sense of right and responsibility and makes him wish "the world to be in uniform and at a sort of moral attention for ever". (p.2)

In expressing his final vision in images of order, he voices Fitzgerald's sense of need for the 'fundamental decencies" in life. Nick, the narrator of the novel, is also the seer – that participant as well as the observer – who while narrating the events and actions becomes also involed in it. As he says: "I was within and without, simultaneously enchanted and repelled by the inexhaustible variety of life". (p. 36)

He serves the role of the detached moralist. While admiring the romantic naivete and the colossal vitality of Gatsby's illusion he observes as well as examines the nature and the motives of the different characters in the novel. He evalutes his own disillusioning experience in the East. But however disenchanted he may be, he affirms the greatness of Gatsby's romantic quest and tragic failure. The famous final passage of *The Great Gatsby* brings out his idea that dreams are imperishable and are renewed again and again. In Gatsby's humanity, Nick discovers man's essential capacity to hope in the face of hopelessness. He epitomizes his firm faith: "Gatsby believed in the green light, the orgiastic future that year by year recedes before us. It eluded us then, but that's no matter – tomorrow we will run faster, stretch out our arms farther. . . And one fine morning –

> So we beat on, boats against the current, borne back ceaselessly into the past. (p.182)

The Great Gatsby ultimately asserts the value of human order in defiance of everything that defeats it. It opens a 'single window' on the 'inexhaustible variety of life', a unified perspective in the condition of man in his multiverse. Thus *The Great Gatsby* is not simply a chronicle of the Jazz Age or of the Lost Generation but rather a dramatization of the betrayal of the native American dream in corrupt society. It is a saga of an innocent abroad that withstands the test of time and transcends the surface glamour of the glittering twenties.

Gatsby is the eternal dreamer, the innocent seeker trying to recapture the idealized youth with its sense of wonder and its trust in life's limitless possibilities. Gatsby's dream ultimately is the dream of a whole nation and his tragedy is the tragedy of the country – the dark republic. That tragedy is, of course, the death of romantic possibility, of hope of all that America once offered to the ambitious, self-reliant man. But Fitzgerald's success lies in his ability to transform Gatsby's dream into 'human dream'. In a wider sense, the 'attitudes, aspirations, and destinies' in many ways typical of the American experiences are actually part of the experience of the universal man. Jay Gatsby's story unfolds the traditional motive of American experience divided between the yearning for innocence and the bitter experiences of the rude reality, between the idyllic vision of the West and the tainted urbanity of the East, between the eternal quest for the 'Chosen land' and the ever-receding 'green light'.

In this novel Fitzgerald's maturity of vision lies in the objective rendering of the intensely personal experience into a general one. Here he attains that "ability to hold two opposed ideas in the mind at the same time and still retain the ability to function".[11]

The Great Gatsby reveals the maturity of the artistic craftmanship of Scott Fitzgerald. The 'magic suggestiveness' of its highly refined and mature prose, the poetic language and controlled diction of it – all together successfully convey the melancholy sadness of Gatsby's tragedy.

With *The Great Gatsby* F. Scott Fitzgerald created his own vision of national tragedy and of high art. From the early moment of intellectual naivety and emotional uncertainty he had come a long way in his literary career to reach the phase of self-fulfilment and self-creation as an artist.

The greatness of *The Great Gatsby* lies in Fitzgerald's ability to reveal the tragic implication of the American dream. Successfully he organized the plot around an agonizing conflict of the moral and social order and enlarged its meaning on the symbolic level of legend and myth. The story rooted in an objective frame of reference represent the irony of American history and the failure of the American dream. *The Great Gatsby* dramatizes the age-old ambiguity between materialism and idealism directly in the life of Jay Gatsby and retrospectively by a glance at history at the end of the novel.

As in his earlier works here also Fitzgerald grappled with some social and moral problems of contemporary life and the novel has its interest as a record of contemporary manners. But here again Fitzgerald the social historian is dominated by Fitzgerald the romantic and the moral commentator. It is totally baseless to charge him as Mencken did of depicting merely "the florid show of modern American life – and especially the devil's dance that goes on at the top". Mencken added further,". . . what engrosses him is the high carnival of those who have too much money to spend and too much time for the spending of it".[12] Much can be said against this. But let us simply refer to the widely accepted fact that Gatsby's story transcends the limits of the time he belonged to. Gatsby stands for eternally recurring man's hope for 'a brave new world'. His tragic awakening symbolizes the disenchantment of mankind as a whole. The fullness of Fitzgerald's living experience of his own society and time enables him to visualise the human destiny in Gatsby's tragedy. *The Great Gatsby* carries its social values and historical perspective into a wider realm of universal symbols. Fitzgerald is able to take the given moment of history as something more than a mere circumstance and to seize the given moment as a moral fact. His sense of wonder and purity of imagination make him 'the poet of borrowed time' and his creation a 'tragic pastoral'. In the words of Arthur Mizener: "Here (*The Great Gatsby*) Fitzgerald's view of his material is completely adequate to his feeling about human experience in general, the life of the people he knows has become the fully rounded particular case for the expression of his whole understanding".[13]

Lionel Trilling in his book, *The Liberal Imagination,* observed: "Gatsby divided between power and dream, comes inevitably to stand for America itself".[14] The subject of American morality is explored historically through the conflict between the surviving Puritan morality of the West and the post-war hedonism of the East; *The Great Gatsby,* both in its action and in its characters embodies 'attitudes, aspirations, and destinies' typical of the American experience. But the lasting significance of this creation owes to its universal implication and as pointed by Maxwell Perkins, the novel imparts 'a sense of eternity'. He acclaims: "It is an extraordinary book, suggestive of all sorts of thoughts and moods".[15] Its theme is the unending quest of the romantic dream which is forever betrayed, in fact and yet redeemed in man's mind. It conveys the mature realization of the writer that the true charm of romantic ideal lies in its remoteness from actuality. Fitzgerald achieves a unique balance between his thought and style and his aesthetic ideal harmonizes with skilled craftsmanship. The very structure of the book is rhythmic and dramatic; it is perfectly balanced and rounded-off. Considering its thematic richness and the method of presentation, its amplitude of meaning and the intensity of impression we can easily realize the significance of T.S. Eliot's well-known statement about the novel – that *The Great Gatsby* was "the first step that American fiction has taken since Henry James. . . . "[16]

Fitzgerald divided the material into nine brief chapters. The first four chapters act as a slow introduction to the climax in the fifty chapter – the 'dead middle of book' as he called it. The last four chapters mark the development of the story to its tragic conclusion at a quickened pace. In this brief span, by a masterful use of technical devices like fore-shortening the dramatic scene, the narrator, the mutual interdependence of character and incident – the events of a single summer and the facts that precede them are encompassed. The narrator's voice in first-person form, a technique adopted from Conrad, introduces and concludes the story. The narrator does not begin at the beginning of hero's life and narrate it chronologically to the end. Rather Nick Carraway starts the story with a strong impression about Gatsby and then takes the readers backwards and forward over his past to provide a fuller basis for their understanding. The narrator who is very much near the centre of things participates in as well as comments on the incidents that take place in course of action. The different characters and events are filtered through the eyes of this narrator. In the process it produces the writer's detachment of vision and gives an objective rendering of the fact. The constant interference of the author's own person that marked the earlier works of Fitzgerald is no more present here. With the help of a narrator Fitzgerald achieves an aesthetic distance and gives voice to the dual aspect of his vision. In order to get a true picture of the human experience that Fitzgerald intends to do in it, one must think of Gatsby and Nick together. If Gatsby represents innocence, dream, imagination and eternity, Nick stands for reason, experience, reality and history. In other words, it presents both the romantic wonder and the realistic judgment of Scott Fitzgerald.

Fitzgerald's artistry in *The Great Gatsby* becomes supreme for the superior quality of its language. It is highly refined and mature, rhythmic, sober and suggestive. It is controlled in its diction but rich in its effectiveness. Lionel Trilling observed: "In Fitzgerald's work the voice of his prose is of the essence of his success. We hear in it at once the tenderness toward human desire that modifies a true firmness of moral judgment".[17] His natural sentences make the reader hear, feel and above all else, see. Fitzgerald believed: "Nobody ever became a writer just by wanting to be one. If you have anything to say, anything you feel nobody has said ever before, you have got to feel it so desperately that you will find some way to say it that nobody has ever found before, so that the thing you have to say and the way of saying it blend as one matter — as indissolubly as if they were conceived together. . . ."[18] In *The Great Gatsby* Fitzgerald achieves this perfect harmony between his style and subject-matter. Like a true creative artist he succeeds in giving voice to his 'sharp and concise attitude about life'.

References

1. Marius Bewley, "Scott Fitzgerald and the Collapse of the American Dream", *The Eccentric Design*, New York: Columbia University Press, 1963, p. 263.
2. Andrew Turnbull, *Scott Fitzgerald*, Penguin Books, 1962, p. 154.
3. *Ibid.*, p. 142.
4. F. Scott Fitzgerald to Maxwell Perkins as quoted in Arthur Mizener's *The Far Side of Paradise*, Boston: Houghton Mifflin Company, 1965, p. 184.
5. Andrew Turnbull, *Scott Fitzgerald*, p. 157.
6. F. Scott Fitzgerald, "Winter Dreams", *The Stories of F. Scott Fitzgerald* (Introduction by Malcolm Cowley), New York: Scribner's, 1969, p. 145.
7. F. Scott Fitzgerald, "The Sensible Thing", *The Stories of F. Scott Fitzgerald*, p. 156.
8. *Ibid.*, p. 158.
9. F. Scott Fitzgerald, *The Great Gatsby*, New York: Scribner's, 1953, p. 112.
10. Marius Bewley, "Scott Fitzgerald and the Collapse of American Dream", *The Eccentric Design*, p. 278.
11. F. Scott Fitzgerald, *The Crack-Up*, (ed. by Edmund Wilson) New York: New Directions Paperbook, 1956, p. 69.
12. H. L. Mencken, "The Great Gatsby", Alfred Kazin (ed.), *F. Scott Fitzgerald: The Man and His Work*, New York: Collier Books, 1966, p. 92.
13. Arthur Mizener, "The Poet of Borrowed Time", Alfred Kazin (ed.),

F. Scott Fitzgerald: The Man and His Work, p. 26.

14. Lionel Trilling, "F. Scott Fitzgerald", *The Liberal Imagination*, London, Secker and Warburg, 1951, p. 251.

15. Maxwell E. Perkins, "A Letter on The Great Gatsby", Alfred Kazin (ed.), *F. Scott Fitzgerald : The Man and His Work*, p. 85.

16. T. S. Eliot, "A Letter on The Great Garsby", Alfred Kazin (ed.), *F. Scott Fitzgerald: The Man and His Work*, p. 93.

17. Lionel Trilling, *The Liberal Imagination*, p. 253.

18. F. Scott Fitzgerald, (ed. by Edmund Wilson), *The Crack-Up*, New York: New Directions Paperbook, 1945, pp. 303-4.

9

Tender is the Night
The Imagery of Disorder

THE long time lapse between the publication of *The Great Gatsby* (1925) and the publication of *Tender is the Night* (1934) was a period of silence and literary inactivity of Fitzgerald. His wife's illness and her eventual hospitalization, his psychological strain and financial obligations – were responsible for such inactivity. The sense of instability and bewilderment after the ruinous collapse of the 'Golden Twenties' disturbed his tranquillity of mind. The writer had to find new sources of inspiration in the painful experiences of those sad years. Like Nick Carraway he could state: "I was thirty. Before me stretched the portentous, menacing road of a new decade."[1] But Fitzgerald with his unflagging commitment and stubborn dedication to his craft continued his search for new subjects and experiment with new techniques. At the end of nine long years his new novel *Tender is the Night* appeared showing an unquestionable continuity of themes and inspirations. Even in the complexity of its motives and the varierty of its thematic variations the informing idea seems to be the same as in the preceding novel. What Fitzgerald is concerned with is a presentation of the glittering golden world, its effect on the yearning, searching American – on the innocent, expectant idealist. The theme is once more provided by the concept of the young sentimental idealist corrupted and ruined by contact with the carelessness and selfishness of the leisure class.

Fitzgerald prepared a long preliminary sketch for *Tender is the Night* – 'General Plan' – where be stated: "The novel should do this. Show a man who is a natural idealist, a spoiled priest, giving in for various causes to the ideas of the haute bourgeoisie, and in his rise to the top of the social world losing his idealism, his talent and turning to drink and dissipation. Background one in which the leisure class is at their truly most brilliant and glamorous such as Murphys."[2] Gerald and Sara Murphy with their charm, their wealth, their social elegance and easy manner impressed Fitzgerald deeply. Fitzgerald drew on Gerald Murphy for these characteristics in Dick Diver. But like Gatsby, Dick Diver too started as one man and then changed into his creator's self – changed so completely that Dick's fate was a prophecy of what would happen to the author himself.

Tender is the Night bristles with episodes and characters, in order to give the 'picture' of a whole world. A group of characters is set in a well-defined social situation, and their gradual developments and psychological reactions are followed closely in the novel. The incestuous father; the schizophrenic Nicole; the frigid Baby Warren; the alcoholic Abe North; the homosexuals Campion and Dumphry; the lover Tommy Barban; all these characters are viewed by Rosemary Hoyt, who is innocent and apparently healthy, although dominated by her mother and by Hollywood to the degree that she has not yet lived according to adult standards. Rosemary's angle of vision dominates the book to a great extent and her very presence acts as a catalyst in the general drama of the life of Divers.

At the centre of a whole group of people on the Riviera surrounded by their weaknesses and problems, is Dick Diver, who has inherited 'good instincts, honour, courtesy and courage'. He is a 'superman in possibilities' a man of imagination with the innnate capacity for romantic wornder, an 'organizer of private gaiety, curator of richly incrusted happiness'. Dick has inherited from his father the 'somewhat conscious good manners of the young Southerner coming north after Civil War' and he does maintain them; but he shows overt weakness towards the end of the novel, even his charm becomes ineffectual, as Fitzgerald explicitly defines the nature of his tragedy: "The change came a long way back", Dick confesses to Rosemary, "but at first it didn't show. The manner remains intact for sometime after the morale cracks".[3]

But the great advance in *Tender is the Night* lies in Fitzgerald's conception of Dick Diver. Like Gatsby he is an idealist; and like Gatsby he has great self-confidence, he thinks of himself heroically. Through his manners he creates a world of romantic dreams. Unlike Gatsby, Dick is by training and by temperament self-conscious. He is conscious of his contraries, aware of the dissimulation behind his magical, creative role. Dick is mordibly aware of his developing tragedy, although he can do nothing to prevent it; unlike Gatsby, his tragedy is not only symbolic in its significance but personal as well – one always feels the human consequences in *Tender is the Night*. "Wanting above all to be brave and kind, he had wanted even more than that, to be loved. So it had been. So it would ever be, he saw . . ."[4] This reflection, which occurs directly before the Divers' decision to separate, is merely one of Dick's final perceptions about himself; indeed the haunting aspect of his deterioration is that he can diagnose it so accurately, he can bring to bear the sensitivity of the psychiatrist and yet remain impotent.

Dr. Richard Diver is a brilliant psychiatrist whose life is ruined because he falls in love with the wrong woman and marries her. He commits himself to the exacting task that will embitter his life and ruin his career. As a psychiatrist he knows the pattern which Nicole's life will follow, he knows what marriage to her would mean. Moreover, to make certain that there is no illusion, his colleagues and mentors, Franz and Dohmler are there to tell him bluntly that he must break with her. When they force him to face the fact that Nicole is in love with him and that this 'transference' must be terminated if she is to be spared what might appear as a trgedy to her, he admits that he is half in love with her and that the question of marrying her has passed through his mind. Franz exclaims:"What! And devote half your life to being doctor and nurse and all – never! I know what these cases are. One time in twenty it's finished in the first push – better never see her again !"[5] Dohmler agrees and they work out a plan for what Dick must do, 'he must be most kind and yet eliminate himself'.

Dick attempts the break but cannot go as far with it as he had intended because of the agony of watching the stricken girl as her 'flimsy and scarcely created world' goes to pieces. He is puzzled and distraught as he leaves the hospital and returns to Zurich, and the next weeks are filled with a vast dissatisfaction: "The pathological origin and mechanistic defeat of the affair left a flat and metallic taste. Nicole's emotions had been used unfairly – what if they turned out to have been his own?"[6]

At the sight of her once in a car, as he walked down the street in Zurich, "the air around him was loud with the circlings of all the goblins on the Gross-Munster". He goes home and tries "to write the matter out of his mind in a memorandum that went into detail as to the solemn regime before her", but it is a "memorandum that would have been convincing to any one save to him had written it".[7] He knows how deeply his emotions are involved. He attempts to find antidotes. He is all too aware that 'the logic of his life tended away from the girl'. But after encountering her on a trip to the mountains and riding back to Zurich with her on the train from Caux, he knows that "her problem was one they had together for good now".[8] His need for love (the tragic flaw in his character) and his altruism drives him to marry her. He takes up the double task of being a husband and a physician at the same time.

By marrying Nicole, the promising scientist, enters the world of the haute bourgeoisie – the world which hides under its economic power, selfishness and moral insensibility, corruption, and carelessness. Dick unwarily lets himself be drawn into the orbit of Nicole and compromises his strength and professional ability.

"He had been swallowed up like a gigolo and had somehow permitted his arsenal to be locked up in the Warren safety-deposit vaults."[9] Dick realizes too late how much his own self has been trapped in the net of Nicole's wealth and her illness. He remembers the crass hardness of Baby Warren's statement. "We own you, and you'll admit it sooner or later. It is absurd to keep up the pretense of independence."[10] To them Dick was merely one of "the young doctors that could be purchased in the intellectual stockyards of the South side of Chicago".[11]

To come back to the story, the marriage seems successful, but Nicole, as we learn gradually, has gone through two or three collapses. Dick realizes that the difficulty of taking care of her is more than he had imagined. The psychological tension imposed on him by his double task of being a husband and a doctor gradually breaks him into pieces. When he moves to the Riviera, his abdication becomes irreversible, and he realizes sadly that he has become a mere instrument in a game.

But in the eyes of Rosemary Hoyt, the young actress who now arrives on the scene, Divers' life seems perfect and enviable. She is attracted by the glamour and enthusiasm that seems to surround them in their circle of chosen and fashionable friends. Rosemary, a 'simple' child with her 'immature mind', cannot perceive the inner tension that threatens to break-up their union.

> Her naivete responded whole-heartedly to the expensive simplicity of the Divers, unaware of its complexity and its lack of innocence, unaware that it was all a selection of quality rather than quantity from the run of the world's bazzar, and that the simplicity of behaviour also, the nursery-like peace and good will, the emphasis on the simpler virtues, was part of a desperate bargin with the gods and had been attained through struggles she could not have guessed at. At the moment the Divers represented externally the exact furthermost evolution of a class, so that most people seemed awkward beside them – in

reality a qualitative change had already set in that was not at all apparent to Rosemary.[12]

The young girl dazzled by brilliance of the Divers and her admiration for Dick cannot see the horror that lies behind the fascinating facade of their life on the Riviera. To Rosemary, naive and romantic, Dick Diver's world takes on the aura of a mystic, magical place – from a pebble pile he had made a 'bright tan prayer rug of a beach', and when she ascends to the Villa Diana above, Rosemary feels she has reached the centre of the world. To her Dick "seemed kind and charming – his voice promised that he would take care of her, . . . he would open up whole new worlds for her, unroll an endless succession of magnificent possibilities."[13]

Dick Diver too finds in Rosemary 'the only girl' that he had seen for a long time who 'actually did look like something blooming'.[14] She blooms for him, as her name signifies, as a symbol of remembrance, the dreams, the ambitions, the creative energy of his youth. Rosemary becomes his only hope for rebirth and liberation. She recalls Dick to his youth, makes him see how false his present life is. And the past to which Rosemary returns Dick, is past of the adolescent – 'One of a Tarkington's adolescents' with the 'fatuousness' and jealous pain of youthful desires.

The party in the Villa Diana provides occasion for the exposition of the love affair between Dick and Rosemary. It develops through different episodes like their trip to Paris, their visit to the battlefield, their kiss in the taxicab and so on. At the battlefield near Amiens, he tells Rosemary that the 'whole-souled sentimental equipment' of the past generations was all spent in World War I. In this connection it may be pointed out that at both the beginning and end of this battlefield episode Fitzgerald emphasizes Rosemary's significance by placing her beside the memory of World War I. Dick in his conversation with Rosemary recollects the irreparable past of his own as well as that of the older America of virtues and graciousness. "All my beautiful lovely safe world blew itself up here with a great gust of high explosive love", Dick mourns persistently, "The silver cord is cut and the golden bowl is broken and all that, but an old romantic like me can't do anything about it."[15] Thus Rosemary brings back the memories of his own youth. The only fresh innocence Dick can see anywhere, exists only in the youthful past, in the memory of the illusions of the future that existed in the past – and like Rosemary, the new world is in the process of shedding its youth.

But Rosemary's vitality is the vitality of a growing and dynamic industry. She is "the product of her mother's loving . . . embodying all the immaturity of the race, cutting a new cardboard paper doll to pass before its empty harlot's mind."[16] Dick Diver's generation is older than Rosemary's, and he is a product of older instincts,'honour, courtesy, and courage'. Rosemary is the product of Hollywood – manifesting the effects of Hollywood sentimentality and meretriciousness on the powers of American imagination. In embracing Rosemary, therefore, Dick Diver epitomizes the fall of all idealists from a disciplined and dedicated life to a life of self-indulgence, dissipation, and moral anarchy – a symbol of the parent generation infatuated with its own offspring.

Even aside from Dick's relationship with Rosemary, there are many hints that he is gradually shifting allegiance from the past culture of his father to an unworthy future. In the beginning, he exhhibits dignity and self-discipline, unfailing courtesy, and a firm, if unexpressed, moral code. Before the novel is over, he has been beaten in a brawl with taxi-drivers, has insulted his friend, Mary Minghetti, and at the very end, has been forced to leave Lockport, New York, because he became entangled with a girl who worked in a grocery store. To clarify this change, Fitzgerald underlines it in several passages. The most memorable example is Dick's remark at his father's grave, "Good-bye my father . . . good-bye, all my fathers", signifying his rejection of his father's world, the aristocratic and 'conscious good manners of the young southerner'. Later, as he enters the steamship to return to Europe, he is described as hurrying from the past into the future. But this is only his formal farewell to something he has long since left behind. His attempt to visit Rosemary at her studio is explicitly labelled 'an overthrowing of his past'. And on the following day, in the hotel dining room, although Dick sees in the gold-star mothers 'all the maturity of an older America', and remembers his father and his 'old loyalties and devotions', he turns back to Rosemary and Nicole, the "whole new world in which he believed".[17]

Early in their relationship, when Rosemary begs Dick to take her and he refuses, he attempts to tell her something of what his love for Nicole means, an attempt foredoomed to failure. He makes it clear that it is not a 'cooled relation' as thought by her, rather an 'active love', 'more complicated' than she thinks. Indeed, Dick's love for Nicole is great – a sacrificial love that knows that it is sacrificing. It is only if we understand the greatness of his love that we can understand the tragic proportions of the dilemma with which he is faced. If he is to save her, he must give her up. This is the knowledge which Dick Diver the psychiatrist must carry with him perhaps from the moment he decides to marry Nicole. Certainly it is a knowedge which he must face squarely long before the break is accomplished.

We get one clear indication of the professional side of his relationship to Nicole following her collapse in Paris as result of the murder of the Negro and the appearance of his body in Rosemary's room: "It prophesied possibly a new cycle, a new pause' of the malady."[18] Having gone through unprofessional agonies during her long relapse following Topsy's birth, he had, perforce, hardened himself about her, making a cleavage between Nicole sick and Nicole well. This made it difficult now to disntinguish between his self-protective professional detachment and some new coldness in his heart. "As an indifference cherished, or left to atrophy, becomes an emptiness, to this extent he had learned to become empty of Nicole, serving her against his will with negations and emotional neglect."[19]

And it is against his will that he continues to serve her by forcing her step by painful step to a completeness that can come only with independence of him. His love for her cries out to him to protect her, to shield her, to support her. At the same time his love is great enough to make him do what he knows he must do if she is ever to be a whole person again: "Many times he had tried unsuccessfully to let go his hold on her . . . but always when he turned away from her into himself he left her holding Nothing in her hands and starting at it, calling it many names, but knowing it was only the hope that he would come back soon."[20]

This is the torment which racks him as he continues in his double role of Dick Diver, husband, and Dr. Richard Diver, psychiatrist. It is stated explicitly after Nicole's running away from him and the children at the Agiri Fair. Recovering, she begs, 'Help me, help me, Dick !' A wave of agony went over him. It was aweful that such a fine tower should not be erected, only suspended, suspended from him."[21] It is Tommy Barban who becomes the final instrument of release. And Dick knows it even before Nicole does – knows it, fights his inward battle and comes out the victor and the loser.

Nicole is vaguely aware that something beyond her understanding and beyond her control is developing. She senses what it is willed by her husband and forced inexorably to its conclusion as he drains his own heart's blood to give her life. "It was as though an incalculable story was telling itself inside him, about which she could only guess in the moments when it broke through the surface."[22]

Nicole is happy knowing that two men, Dick and Tommy, are in a sense in combat for her: "She did not want anything to happen, but only for the situation to remain in suspension as the two men tossed her from one mind to another; she had not existed for a long time, even as a ball."[23] She begins to think of an affair with Tommy. "If she need not, in her spirit, be forever one with Dick as he had appeared last night, she must be something in addition, not just an image on his mind, condemned to endless parades around the circumference of a medal."[24] She has reached the first real point of independence. For the first time she can defy Dick. A transference of Dick's vitality – both physical and spiritual, fills the void in her personality and restores her universe.

As Nicole comes gradually to realization that she is almost complete, a new sense of freedom develops within her: "She had a sense of being cured and in a new way. Her ego began blooming like a great rich rose as she scrambled back along the labyrinths in which she had wandered for years."[25] She feels that now she can stand alone without Dick. She feels like a happy child. But she knows that she has betrayed Dick – his love – and a sense of deep remorse assails her mind. She approaches Dick's sanctuary and finds him absorbed in thought.

> He was thinking, he was living a world completely his own, and in the small motions of his face, the brow raised or lowered, the eyes narrowed or widened, the lips set and reset, the play of his hands, she saw him progress from phase to phase of his own story spinning out inside him, his own, not hers. Once he clenched his fists and leaned forward, once it brought into this face an expression of torment and despair – when this passed its stamp lingered in his eyes. For almost the first time in her life she was sorry for him – it is hard for those who have once been mentally afflicted to be sorry for those who are well, and though Nicole often paid lip service to the fact that he had led her back to the world she had forefeited, she had thought of him really as an inexhaustible energy, incapable of fatigue – she forgot the troubles she caused him at the moment when she forgot the troubles of her own that had prompted her. That he no longer controlled her – did he know that? Had he willed it all?[26]

The case is finished. Dr. Diver is at liberty. But the toll has been too much for Dick. He is exhausted both as a physician and as a man. He is sapped, drained emotionally. His energy, his strength, his love have been expended in the one passion of his life. 'The layer of hardness in him, of self-control and of self-discipline' which Rosemary had felt in him at their first meeting had served him well. It will serve him still as he moves from one small town practice to another, but it cannot wipe out what has been or compensate for what can never be again.

He has succeeded in his task, but has been defeated in life. He disappears from the scene ending in a melancholy provincial anonymity – "his latest note was post-marked from Hornell, New York, which is some distance from Geneva and a very small town; in any case he is almost certainly in that section of the country, in one town or another."[27] The new world is too powerful for him. He cannot shape it according to the ABCs of the human decency, he had learned from his father and his own attempt to transmit the good heritage becomes corrupted and futile.

Such a reading obviously makes Dick Diver a more admirable character and a more heroic one. His story assumes the diimensions of tragedy of one who accepts his choice to marry Nicole and his choice to free her is deliberately made because of his love for her. But Fitzgerald is too good a writer to make it quite that simple. He is aware of the complexities of human motivations and personal relationships. He makes his character believable by showing the less admirable qualities in him and the selfish motives which complicate the altruistic. A conscious decision to marry a mental patient, to devote one's life to her cure; a calculated plan to force her to renounce her saviour – this is too cold, too incredible, too inhuman. The choices must be blurred, must he softened, nust be less starkly rational.

We are told before Dick knows whether he will marry Nicole or not, before he has to make any decision about her, something about his nature which is crucial to an understanding of his subsequent actions: "In the dead white hours in Zurich staring into a stranger's pantry across the upshine of a street-lamp, he used to think that he wanted to be good, he wanted to be kind, he wanted to be brave and wise, but it was all pretty difficult. He wanted to be loved, too, if he could fit it in."[28] And in a passage which comes, significantly, immediately after the final break with Nicole, the passage in which she gains completeness and with it independence of Dick, he receives a telephone call at 2 O'clock in the morning and responds to it by going to Antibes to help Mary North and Caroline Sibly-Biers get out of jail – two women whom he despises and who have publicly humiliated him. His response is described in these words:

> He got up and, as he absorbed the situation, his self-knowledge assured him that he would undertake to deal with it – the old fatal pleasingness, the old forceful charm, swept back with its cry of "Use me !" He would have to go fix this thing that he didn't care a damn about, because it has early become a habit to be loved, perhaps from the moment when he had realized that he was the last hope of a decaying clan. On an almost parallel occasion, back in Dohmler's clinic on the Zurichsee, realizing this power, he had made his choice, chosen Ophelia, chosen the sweet poison and drunk it.[29]

This desire to be 'brave and kind' and 'to be loved' – a great desire no doubt – forms the fatal weakness in Dick which underlies the pattern of his life. There is an incompleteness in him which is covered over by the charm which he has cultivated that used to draw people to him, to sweep them up and manipulate them, to use himself to attempt their fulfilment. "He was condemned to carry with him the egos of certain people, early met and early loved, and to be only as complete as they were complete themselves."[30] But it is this very complexity of character and of motive that takes Dick to a heightened level of tragedy.

Dick's tragic flaw, then is, in himself: his destiny is of his own making. Yet his flaw is the flaw of a society. Just as Nicole is, so Dick too is the product and representive of a whole social class when he sets out on his mission to be good and to do good, he carries with him the illusions and weaknesses of a whole nation: " — the illusions of eternal strength and health, and of the essential goodness of people — they were the illusions of a nation, the lies of generations of frontier mothers who had to croon falsely that there were no wolves outside the cabin door."[31] Dick has met the wolves in the Warrens and their ducal family, their world of hidden perfidy and irresponsible carelessness. Thus his adventure symbolizes the doom of all idealists, the innocent Americans who wishing to be 'too close to the line' are only to be wrecked on the beaches of Europe and to rerturn beaten to their 'cabins'.

Tender is the Night ends thus without the promise of a new beginning. It depicts not only the, 'intricate destiny' of Dr. Richard Diver, the decline of an idealistic American, but the death of American idealism and innocence. Here the death of idealism occurs when life seems to be at its ripest, in the hot Riviera Sun, or at night among parties where charming, talented people scarcely conceal their crippled natures, where illness and health seem almost indistinguishable from one another. Once more the Fitzgeraldian hero transcends the work of 'here and now' and foreshadows a complex parable as in *The Great Gatsby*.

In *Tender is the Night* Fitzgerald fulfilled his ambition to write a novel that would be 'the model for the age'. He poured all the passions of his social discontent and historical understandintg into it. With this "philosophical, now called psychological, novel", a novel full of beautiful and sad emotions, Fitzgerald moved away from universal myths and toward the pathos of history. In *Tender is the Night* Fitzgerald created a work of fiction uniting romantic beauty with historical and social depth. He represented Dick as a man in action and in conflict in a definite social order and saw him not as a mere individual but as a social being. He made Dick succumb to the psychological and social pressures, to an array of disrupting forces exactly as a social being. The failure of society is manifested in that of an individual who embodied its graces and weaknesses. Thus the novel is a vision in art of an era in American history pervaded with moral anarchy and imagery of disorder.

Tender is the Night composed between 1925 and 1934, went through three versions and numerous titles. Fitzgerald once remarked that he had written more than 400,000 words on it, but had thrown away three-fourths. Even after the publication he worked hard on it to replace the original flash-back structure and present the story in chronological order. He made these drastic revisions and replanning out of his strong conviction about serious writings. On 4 March 1938, he commented to Mr. Dayton Kohler: "The necessity of the artist in every generation has been to give his work permanence in every way by a safe shaping and a constant pruning, lest he be confused with the journalistic material that has attracted lesser men".[32] How seriously Fitzgerald adhered to his standards for the art of fiction is well demonstrated in the constant 'shaping' and 'pruning' of his material in *Tender is the Night*.

Fitzgerald wished to make this new novel a work of incomparable artistry so that it could serve as "the model for the age that Joyce and Stein are searching for, that Conrad didn't find". (*Letters*, p. 182) The nine year gap between *The Great Gatsby* and *Tender is the Night* is not then, as often has been considered, an ignominous failure of the author. Rather it is marked with his sincere and ceaseless effort to work out a new conception of his material. The strains of his life as an artist and an intellectual over the years from 1926 to 1932 – not to speak of his personal and social life – were exceptionally intense. He was caught into a cross-fire of conflicting intentions. He had no real conception of what such a novel would be like; only had the feelings of how it ought to be. He was going through a painful process of growth and an artist's growth is no more smooth than the path of any interior development. There was a sound principle behind his ambition to be a great writer. He wanted not merely to succeed greatly, but also to do better. The qualities of mind that had enabled him to grow beyond *This Side of Paradise* and *The Beautiful and Damned* now prompted him to grow beyond *The Great Gatsby.*

Like Amory Blaine, with Fitzgerald too, "it was always the becoming he dreamed of, never the being".[33] He could realize how gradually his literary fame was getting eclipsed by the rising reputation of his contemporary, Ernest Hemingway. He knew also how his long silence made his friends and critics sceptical about his literary worth. Even Zelda Fitzgerald whose habits had often hindered her husband's writings in the past took this lapse to be waste and dissipation. In a letter to his generous literary agent Harold Ober Fitzgerald gave expression to his wounded feelings and a sense of firm resolution. He wrote: "I know you're losing faith in me, and Max too, but God knows one has to rely in the end on one's own judgment. I could have published four lousy, half-baked books in the last five years and people would have thought I was at least a worthy young man not drinking myself to pieces in the South Seas – but I'd be dead as Michael Arlen, Bromfield, Tom Boyd, Callaghan and the others who think they can trick the world with the hurried and the second rate". (*Letters,* p. 395) In another letter to Maxwell Perkins he wrote almost the same word: "I wrote young and I wrote a lot and the pot takes longer to fill up now, but the novel, my novel is a different matter than if I'd hurriedly finished it up a year and a half ago. . . . *I know what I'm doing* – honestly Max. . . . 'He's through' is an easy cry to raise but its safer for the critics to raise it – at the evidence in print than at a long silence". (*Letters,* pp. 221-22)

A process of becoming, a principle of growth in intellect and art created the form for Scott Fitzgerald's development from *The Great Gatsby* to *Tender is the Night*. This novel may fall short of high level of performance that *Gatsby* achieved. But this book, as Wright Morris points out, "is wiser, consciously wiser; the sun that had been rising is now setting, and Dick Diver is plainly stigmatized with the author's sense of his own predicament. . . . Dick Diver, having had his enchantment, having listened to the dream that pandered in whispers, and having been compelled to an aesthetic contemplation he has finally come to understand . . . that the future now stands behind him, with its tail in its mouth.[34] So Dick drifts from Buffalo to Batavia, from Geneva, New York to Hornell where that dream of love (Nicole) finally lost track of him. He is deposited in a limbo where there is neither a past nor a future.

With *Tender is the Night* Fitzgerald achieves a mature understanding of the relation of the individual to society, of the nature of good and evil. He acquires a coherent grasp of social forces and presents the dramatic conflict and ruin of the hero in a clearly defined frame of reference. The conflict between Dick Diver's radiant idealism and hypocrisy of 'haute bourgeoisie' reveals Fitzgerald's success to illustrate and comment on the disintegrating ethical and sociological order. The different characters stand for definite social and moral positions and exemplify in their conflicts a contrast of wider social implications and a larger moral and symbolic significance. And once more the significance of the novel transcends the literal statement to become 'philosophic' and to foreshadow a complex parable of human predicament as in *The Great Gatsby*.

But the fictional methods adopted in *Tender is the Night* are different from those of the former case. In *The Great Gatsby* the symbolic implications sprang from the inner core of single dramatic moments. They were suggested and projected with a technique of rapid allusions, meaningful hints and sudden realizations in a foreshortened perspective. In *Tender is the Night* they are conveyed to the reader through an extensive elucidation, scrupulous documentation and explicit comments. These were perhaps the 'new canons' of 'the philosophical now called psychological, novel' of which Fitzgerald wrote in a letter to John Peale Bishop. Fitzgerald stated that in his new novel he 'was shooting at something like *Vanity Fair*'. (*Letters*, p. 363) He tried to substitute a '*tour de force*' with a 'confession of faith', a sonnet sequence with an epic'. He stated: "There were moments all through the book where I could have pointed up dramatic scenes, and I *deliberately* refrained from doing so because the material itself was so harrowing and highly charged that I did not want to subject reader to a series of nervous shocks. . . ." (*Letters*, p. 363) So instead of a series of dramatic scenes, we get less tense and less compressed rhythm and a slower pace, a kind of epic extension and grandeur. Instead of sudden starts or allusive passages we find a gradual development of the main theme with qualifying and illustrative episodes. All these constitute a shifting from dramatic convention to the pictorial ideal in a typical nineteenth century tradition that Fitzgerald wished to do.

In *Tender is the Night*, though psychological analyses of the characters have predominance, it is always in action that their true natures are revealed. The interplay between incident and character is more complex. Fitzgerald's language here is more complex and more elaborate. It spreads out in descriptions and analyses. Its flow is discursive and spreading. Its pattern is in the form of a long paragraph – slowly developing from sentence to sentence, from period to period. But all the same it retains the delicacy of rhythm depicting the varying moods and reactions of the characters on different occasions. Fitzgerald's 'stylistic mastery' as Sergio Perosa observes, "appears in his slow and measured beginnings, which are worked out to the climax of the scene and then carefully brought to their conclusion, usually with a dying fall or a 'fading away'.[35]

According to Arthur Mizener "the book's defects are insignificant compared to its sustained richness of texture, its sureness of language, the depth and penetration of its understanding – not merely of a small class of people . . . but of the bases of all human disaster. With all its faults, it is Fitzgerald's finest and most serious novel".[36]

If we accept Malcolm Cowley's point of view that a novel has to be judged for what it gives us, not for its defects in execution, then *Tender is the Night* is one of the books that will endure for its lasting emotion and vitality, honesty of feeling and complexity of life. The novel is pervaded with Fitzgerald's fundamental wise and tragic sense of life. It presents Fitzgerald's full exploitation of the most important of all his convictions about experience.

References

1. F. Scott Fitzgerald, *The Great Gatsby*, New York: Scribner's Paperback, 1953, p. 136.
2. F. Scott Fitzgerald, "General Plan" quoted from Arthur Mizener's *The Far Side of Paradise*, Boston: Houghton Mifflin Company, 1965, pp. 345-46.
3. F. Scott Fitzgerald, *Tender is the Night*, New York: Scribner's Paperback, 1951, p. 304.
4. *Ibid.*, p. 321.
5. *Ibid.*, pp. 31-32.
6. *Ibid.*, p. 33.
7. *Ibid.*, p. 38.
8. *Ibid.*, p. 50.
9. *Ibid.*, pp. 218-19.
10. *Ibid.*, p. 193.
11. *Ibid.*, p. 47.
12. *Ibid.*, p. 77.
13. *Ibid.*, p. 72.
14. *Ibid.*, p. 77.
15. *Ibid.*, p. 118.
16. *Ibid.*, p. 130.
17. *Ibid.*, p. 162.
18. *Ibid.*, p. 180.
19. *Ibid.*, pp. 180-81.
20. *Ibid.*, pp. 196-97.
21. *Ibid.*, p. 207.
22. *Ibid.*, p. 286.

23. *Ibid.*, p.. 295.
24. *Ibid.*
25. *Ibid.*, p. 307.
26. *Ibid.*, pp. 318-19.
27. *Ibid.*, p. 334.
28. *Ibid.*, p. 23.
29. *Ibid.*, p. 321.
30. *Ibid.*, p. 263.
31. *Ibid.*, p. 5.
32. F. Scott Fitzgerald, quoted by John Kuehl, "Scott Fitzgerald's Critical Opinions", *Modern Fiction Studies*, Vol. VII, No. 1, Spring, 1961, p. 4.
33. F. Scott Fitzgerald, *This Side of Paradise*, New York: Scribner's, 1970, pp. 17-18.
34. Wright Morris, "The Function of Nostalgia: F. Scott Fitzgerald", Arthur Mizener (ed.), *Twentieth Century Views: F. Scott Fitzgerald*, Englewood Cliffs, N.J., Prentice-Hall, Inc., 1963, pp. 30-31.
35. Sergio Perosa, *The Art of F. Scott Fitzgerald*, Ann Arbor, The University of Michigan Press, 1965, p. 130.
36. Arthur Mizener, *The Far Side of Paradise*, Boston: Houghton Mifflin Company, 1965, p. 267.

10

The Last Tycoon
A Quest for Identity

WITH *Tender is the Night,* a novel of 'confession of faith', Fitzgerald regained his self-esteem and wished to recover lost ground of his literary reputation. But the victory he had gained over himself in this work of art and philosophy was mutilated by unfavourable criticism of the reviewers. *Tender is the Night* failed to re-establish his literary fame that he had enjoyed almost a decade ago. He felt alienated from his contemporaries and was overtaken by sense of neglect and isolation. Life seemed to be a 'process of breaking down' with the blows from outside and within. Apart from this failure of *Tender is the Night,* Zelda's incurable insanity, Fitzgerald's own alcoholism and physical illness, excessive financial presure – took out all his strength and energy and intensified his sense of loss and waste that haunted his spirit all the time. He felt exhausted and suddenly realized that he had "cracked like an old plate".[1] He recorded his gnawing experiences of disintegrating personality in self-revealing essays of *The Crack-Up.*

Fitzgerald's loss of vitality made him feel that life had lost its savour. *The Crack-Up* essays, as he told Maxwell Perkins, revealed the "general eclipse of ambition and determination fortitude" – all the very qualities that he adored most.[2] In his desperate attempts to paste the cracked plate together he discovered: " . . . there was not an 'I' any more – not a basis on which I could organize my self-respect – save my limitless capacity for toil that it seemed I possessed no more. It was strange to have no self – to be like a little boy left alone in a big house, who knew that now he could do anything he wanted to do, but found that there was nothing that he wanted to do – ".[3] He began to realize that for the past few years his life had been drawing on resources that he did not possess and he had mortgaged himself "physically and spiritually up to the hilt".[4] This physical exhaustion and emotional bankruptcy crearted a void in him; a sense of gloom and despair possessed his soul. During that 'real dark night of the soul' when it seemed 'always three O' clock in the morning', he wished "to refuse to face things as long as possible by retiring into an infantile dream. . . hoping that things will adjust themselves by some great material or spiritual bonanza."[5] Later he considered this nervous breakdown of him as a spiritual 'change of life'. He felt: "it was a protest against a new set of conditions I would have to face and a protest of my mind at having to make the psychological adjustments which would have set this new set of circumstances".[6] In short, *The Crack-Up* reveals Fitzgerald's crisis of self-confidence.

The artist in Fitzgerald could not accept this failure of Fitzgerald the man. Fitzgerald always cherished the sacred desire of being an artist and not a careerist. He despised the 'trash writings', the cheap popular magazine fiction that he had to write at different times just to earn a living. So even at this crucial point of his identity-crisis he did not leave his attempt to find out his early self and re-create that golden moment – "when the fulfilled future and the wistful past weer mingled in a single gorgeous moment – when life was literally a dream".[7]

In the role of a screenwriter against the new background of Hollywood, Fitzgerald tried to forget his past failures and get back his lost identity in Monroe Stahr, the hero of his next novel, *The Last Tycoon*. He pursued desperately to pull himself together and re-discover his creative self even in this changed atmosphere that seemed so repulsive and histrionic to him. With the same old powerful imagination and genuine impulse, he tried to create "something new and entirely different" from his earlier works. *The Last Tycoon* happening to be the last of his creation came from the disillusioned artist still believing in the great promises of life. It served to be a sort of poetic as well as personal catharsis to him.

The unfinished manuscript of *The Last Tycoon* shows that Fitzgerald was still trying to fit the pieces of his self-deluded past into a cohernt and functioning whole. Although *The Last Tycoon* describes the growing power of organized labour and Communist infiltration in Hollywood studios, it is more a personal document than a sociological tract; primarily, it is the story of a once-powerful and dominating personality, who, struggling with changing social patterns and with personal confusions and inner conflicts, falls into moral and spiritual bankruptcy. Conceived, as it was, after Fitzgerald's own psychological crack-up, the novel clearly represents not only the struggle with his own self-delusion, but also his final attmept to give shape and meaning to his own identity.

As a writer Fitzgerald's problem was to find the right way of presenting man's loss of identity and moral disintegration artistically. In order to achieve 'the verisimilitude of a first person narrative, combined with a Godlike knowledge of all events that happen to my characters' the story of *The Last Tycoon* is told by an impersonal narrator, a kind of 'centre of revelation' through whom character and action are revealed.[8] While recovering in a tuberculosis sanitarium, Cecilia, daughter of the Hollywood producer Brady, narrates the story of Stahr's rise and fall as she remembers it. She is of the movies, but not in them, a mind of outsider, as Fitzgerald himself had always been. Like other characters, she is a fragment of the writer's personality. A further problem in writing, as the notes indicate, was that of selecting the right name for the characters. Fitzgerald changed the name of the heroine from Thalia to Kathleen. The narrator's father becomes Brady instead of Bradoque. Although the problem of naming is perhaps trivial, it must have bothered Fitzgerald, for he even incorporates it as a major theme of the novel. As Wylie White says, "I didn't feel I had any rightful identity until I got back to the hotel and the clerk handed me a letter addressed to me in my name." (p.11)

It is through the confusion of naming – suggestive of a quest for identity – that Fitzgerald introduces Monroe Stahr as the hero of the novel and reveals through action and symbol the pattern of behaviour which has made Stahr's life one of disintegration and self-delusion. Stahr is actually made known through his friend Schwartz as they return to Hollywood on a transcontinental plane from New York. Although he has known Stahr for a long time, Schwartz cannot recall the name of the man who has taken the bridal suite on the plane. In conversation, he misnames him 'Smith' and warns him to look out for enemies in Hollywood. Once a practical man of decision in the movies, but now a down-and-out producer, Schwartz clearly belongs to a past that Hollywood no longer represents. His face, as the narrator observes, has fallen into its "more disintegrated alignments". (p. 12) When the plane lands at Nashville, Tennessee, Schwartz leaves the airport alone and wanders to the statue of Andrew Jackson, and there commits suicide. Clearly, the self-destruction of a man who believes in the unity and importance of the individual signifies a loss of faith in such values, just as the sacrifice to the shrine of a man famous for his devotion to these ideals signifies continued belief in them. And just as the fall of Schwartz serves as a preview of Stahr's own life, so with Schwartz's death the fictitious 'Smith' is annihilated, and the true identity of Stahr emerges as a normal, integrated, sane personality.

Monroe Stahr, regarded in Hollywood as "the only sound nut in a hatful of cracked ones", (p.19) is basically an artist and creator who directs all his energies to raising the movie industry to an artistic level. Endowed with supreme intelligence, passion and competence for his work he tries to elevate this art form. He takes "the gloom out of a picture and gives it a style".[9] He functions as a leader and supervises the people to get the best out of them. He has a gift of seeing 'below the surface into reality' and that makes him 'their man' and 'the unity' in the organization To sustain this artistic role he has to struggle against the hostility of his enemy groups at work in the movie studioes. In a changing world where his credo of life is no longer valid he has to struggle against the conflict of interests and meet his inevitable failure. His ruin is caused both by the external forces as well as his inner tension – the enemy that lies in his own self-delusion.

The Last Tycoon is, then, the story of Monroe Stahr, a once 'nameless' man, who, at the age of twenty-three, had first climbed his way to success. (Fitzgerald was also twenty-three when he published his first novel). A small man, Stahr has always been a fighter. In his youth he headed a gang in the Bronx. Popular with men, he likes being with the boys; yet he is never one of them. Throughout his life he has always darted in and out of his various roles with dexterity. "If he could go from problem to problem, there was a certain rebirth of vitality with each change." (p.37) Although success has come to him, he remains uncertain and indecisive. Direct and frank by nature, he has never quite known how he 'got to be Mr. Stahr'. As we shall see, Stahr's quest for identity follows a kind of pattern of dying and rebirth, which Fitzgerald's use of flight and plane imagery peculiarly represents.

Introducing the plane trip in the first chapter, Fitzgerald makes the flight metaphor central throughout the novel. He represents Stahr as a man who has flown high to achieve an overview of life in all its complexity. Stahr's whole life has been an 'aerial adventure'. It is flight that has given him vision and insight. Long ago he – "... had flown up very high to see, on strong wings. When he was young. And while he was up there he had looked on all the kingdoms, with the kind of eyes that can stare straight into the sun. Beating his wings tenaciously – finally frantically – and keeping on beating them, he had stayed up there longer than most of us, and then, remembering all he had seen from his great height of how things were, he had settled gradually to earth". (p.20)

In Hollywood – this city of 'mystery and promise' – Stahr achieves position and power. Here he has found a "new way of measuring our jerky hopes and graceful rogueries and awkward sorrow". (p.20) But the flight metaphor, has further meaning . In his note-book Fitzgerald observes that unlike the English, "Americans, restless and with shallow roots, needed fins and wings. There was even a recurrent idea in America about an education that would leave out history and the past, that should be a sort of equipment for aerial adventure, weighed down by none of the stowaways of inheritance or tradition."[10]

Clearly, if up to now Stahr has been able to escape his past, that is, not be burdened by it. Schwartz has not; for is it not inheritance or tradition-Jackson, the monument, that kills him? Flight may save; it has always functioned as a new beginning for Stahr; he has even taken the 'bridal suite' on the plane. But flight also destroys, as in the case of Schwartz. When Stahr returns to Hollywood the 'stowaways of inheritance or tradition' begin to weigh him down.

Stahr loses the city in which he has had his success by a series of blows that are struck from both without and within. Fitzgerald represents the disintegration through symbols. Stahr realizes that something has gone wrong when he discovers that the earthquake, which he has slept through has burst not only the water mains in the studio lot, but also something inside himself. The backlot looks like the "torn picture books of childhood, like fragments of stories dancing in an open fire". (p.25) As he watches the picture of his dead wife drift by on the surface of the water, he realizes with terrible fear that the past as he has known it has vanished. The personal loyalty of workers to an individual has been replaced by an organized union with its own spokesman and organizer. There are 'clay feet everywhere'. These outward signs of destruction and change aptly reflect the disintegration of Stahr's inner self. Confused, alone, he wonders who or what will nurse him back to 'completeness', 'what breast or shrine, what fragment of picture or illusion'. The doctor tells him that he has a heart ailment. He decides that if he is going to die he wants "to stop being Stahr for a while and hunt for love like men who has no gifts to give, like young nameless men who looked along the streets in the dark". (p.90) Although Stahr seeks to obliterate a past that seems to have played him false, he also tries to use that past as a new beginning.

The earthquake that destroyed something in Stahr has also introduced him to love and romance, both of which give an illusion of security to his old identity. From the confusion that was the flooded lot, he remembers having seen two women. When he finally locates them he identifies the wrong one, a girl named Edna Smith, who introduces him, however, to the 'right' one. Kathleen Moore is glamorous, yet "poor, unfotunate, and tagged with a middle-class exterior which doesn't fit in with the grandeur Stahr demands of life". (p.140) He falls in love with her, and like the rest of his past with which she becomes identified, she becomes absolutely necessary to him. As Rosemary was for Dick Diver a promise of new life, so also Kethleen seems to be an anchor for him in his loneliness." He has an overwhelming urge toward the girl, who promises to give life back to him ... she is the heart of hope and freshness."[11] But clearly something has gone wrong. As the error in naming suggests, Stahr is no longer a man of authority and decision. Once he has been mistaken for Smith; now, as if occupying Schwartz's role, he has made the identical error in naming. Like Schwartz, Stahr is losing his grip on life.

If Stahr's new 'aerial adventure' gives an illusion of unity to his life, his 'aerial romance', burdened with obsolete values of a self-deluded past, ends with inevitable failure. Stahr invites Kathleen to his half-finished Malibu beach home; he confesses that he does not have sufficient material at hand to finish the 'fuselage' (p.81) of his new home. The author expresses his feeling in metaphor that uses flight image again. The luxury, the obsolete items of past are there – buit-in book cases, curtain rods, cushioned chairs, a ping-pong table, the trap in the floor for a movie projector – but the household necessities, the sides and the roof, are missing. In this half-built 'new world', Stahr is even now, as the narrator says of him later, playing a "losing battle with his instinct towards schizophrenia". (p.126) Further realization comes when, in front of Kathleen, Stahr makes another error in naming. He believes the telephone call is from the President of the United States, but he has misunderstood. He has actually been speaking to an orang-outang. He knows someone has tricked him, but he tries to go along with the gag: "Hello, orang-outang-God, what a thing to be ! – Do you know your name . . . He doesn't seem to know his name." (pp.83-84) Twice mistaken over names, Stahr is helplessly confused, as if his error in identification reflects his own uncertainty of self. After the seduction Katheleen asks him: "Don't you always think – hope that you'll be one person, and then find you're still two." (p.88) Her question is ironic mockery. Stahr is two persons striving to be one, and Kathleen, to whom he has turned for even the illusion of unity and fulfilment, writes later that she intends to marry someone else.

The episode on the beach, which follows the seduction scene, underlines the growing incapacity of the last tycoon as a topflight Hollywood producer. When Stahr leaves the house, he meets an old Negro, who has really come out to 'read some Emerson', but is busy picking up grunion. (p.92) What bothers Stahr is that the Negro refuses to let his children attend movies. Since the man is a Rosicrucian, Stahr asks if the brotherhood is against pictures. "Seems as if they don't know what they are for", the Negro tells him. "One week they for one thing and next week for another." (p.93) Stahr feels somehow personally responsible for such indecision, as if his own pictures were not 'artistic' enough to merit the sanction of the brotherhood or the attention of a man who is self-reliant, as Stahr is not. Has he not failed in the very exercise of talent that has always sustained him? Are there to be no new flights, except those burdened with a past of self-delusion? Returning to the studios, Stahr is confronted with a new problem: organized labour

– the enemy of individual power and leadership – has struck a blow from the 'outside'.

If Fitzgerald had followed the outline which he had worked out, part of the remaining action of the novel was to show the effect of this conflict on Stahr. The scenes are fragmentary, but nevertheless present Fitzgerald's point of view clearly. Stahr's meeting with Brimmer, the Communist labour organizer, clarifies what Stahr has begun to realize – his loss of personal; power and leadership in the movie industry. The only leadership that Stahr really understands is that of individual triumph, the personal loyalty between employer and employee. At the interview he is white and nervous. He accuses Brimmer of trying to break up the 'unity' in his 'model plant'. Since Stahr is – or has been – that unity, he feels that the Communists are trying to 'get' him personally. Actually, of course, Stahr is right, and when he asks Brimmer, "You don't really think you're going to overthrow the government", and Brimmer replies, "No, Mr. Stahr. But, we think perhaps you are." (p.122) Stahr is clearly reminded of his loss of prestige, his waning power. The interview leaves him weak and confused. The once powerful tycoon seems to be on neither one side nor the other. "The Reds see him now as a conservative – Wall Street as a Red." (p.130)

Whatever the weakness of Stahr's position, Fitzgerald does not side with the Communists. As he writes in 1940, "You can neither cut through, nor challenge nor beat the fact that there is an organized movement over the world before which you and I as individuals are less than the dust."[12] He clearly sees the danger of this "intensely dogmatic and almost mystical religion" to the individual: "Whatever you say", the Communists have ways of twisting it into shapes which put you in some lower category of mankind . . . , and disparage you both intellectually and personally in the process.[13] And through Stahr's position in Hollywood Fitzgerald makes us directly conscious of a class struggle, not as in *Tender is the Night*, where the workers are passive suppliers of leisure-class luxury, but in active terms with the employees as an organized force.

The forces of collectivism put an end to his role as the paternalistic boss. In the words of Bruccoli "he is an anarchronism under attack from both the capitalists and the communists".[14] There are hints that with Stahr's death the movie industry is to be destroyed as a medium for artistry by the unscrupulous forces symbolized in the conscienceless company lawyer, Fleicshacker.

What we can see of *The Last Tycoon* is thus a realistic portrait of Hollywood and the defeat of a brilliant individual who wished to control everything with understanding and intelligence. Hollywood is presented as "a mining town in lotus land" – an American microcosm where the idealistic and artistic impulse is blighted and frustrated by the crude commercialism. It portrays a social milieu with its inherent tragic potentialities in its nature. Fitzgerald depicted this world in all its minutest details, in its mechanics and in its essence. The novel, as Fitzgerald made it quite clear, is certainly not about Hollywood. But surely it occupies a vast portion in the novel indicating its indispensibility for the whole design of and the action in the novel. Through the story of Stahr's defeat against the setting of this business world Fitzgerald once more revealed the symbolic conflict between the two ethical and geographical poles of East and West. In short, Stahr's antagonist Brady is primarily linked with the world of the East – the world of money and ruthless business, the world of Wall Street and competition of brutal and corrupt force. Stahr, on the other hand, tries to give life to his creation – the flowering of art and idealism – in the West.

In a letter to the editor of a magazine in which Fitzgerald hoped to serialize his new novel he wrote: "Unlike *Tender Is The Night*, it is not the story of deterioration – it is not depressing and not morbid in spite of the tragic ending".[15] But ironically enough *The Last Tycoon* is the story of Stahr's defeat, if not deterioration. The analysis of the fragmented scenes show a deep renewal of the theme – the death of a set of values. As in his other novels, here too, the traditional individualism is defeated in part by a section of society devoid of humanistic values and the rest by the inner conflicts of the protagonist himself. Fitzgerald presented Stahr "ruling with a radiance that is almost moribund in its phosphorescence".[16] From the very beginning we see Stahr in a state of decay. He has been warned that his health is undermined, his psyche split. Stahr's directing and organizing activities, as portrayed by Fitzgerald are compulsive rather than controlled and purposeful. Equally compulsive is his love affair – "the meat of the book" (p.139) – his attempt to recapture the past fragrance and to seek a future promise in Kathleen. The lonely young widower with a pervasive sense of loss suffers from indecision to marry her and thereby loses her. Thus Stahr's unhappy love affair, his waning strength and the conflicts both within and without make him feel miserable and embittered towards the end.

Stahr is driven by the logic of situation to fall in with Brady's idea "of setting up a company union". (p.130) Stahr's hostility to unions pushes him into Brady's camp. And the loyalties that lead him to join forces with Brady threaten to destroy the ego and integrity still left in him. Ultimately Stahr is to be shown losing his position in the studio and getting himself entangled in the struggle for power within the industry. This in turn will lead him to resort to methods to blackmail and gengsterism. And then comes the 'recognition scene' to reveal Stahr's self-consciousness: "On the plane he has a reaction of disgust against the course he has taken; he realizes that he has let himself be degraded to the same plane of brutality as Brady". (p.132) Too late he decides to call off the murder since he himself gets crashed in the plane accident before carrying out the decision. This is the pattern of action which Fitzgerald clearly laid down in his outline for the novel, Thus *The Last Tycoon* ends not with "companionship of the Hollywood underdog in a struggle with the racketeers and big producers",[17] rather it dramatizes Stahr's tragic but heroic struggle to save his tattered ego and the remnants of his integrity.

In many ways Stahr is different from Fitzgerald's other heroes.

Whereas they are seen only in their moments of leisure, Stahr is viewed almost exclusively as a working man – work offers the only meaning to a life that has lost all personal significance.

In the words of Bruccoli: "Monroe Stahr is the first hero in a Fitzgerald novel with a succcessful career. Amory and Anthony have no occupations; Gatsby's business activities are shadowy; and Dick Diver abandons his promising career. But Stahr is totally committed to his work and the responsibilities that go with it. He is Fitzgerald's only complete professional."[18] Stahr is a Jewish boy from the Bronx who has risen through his own cunning and diligence, whereas both Gatsbyand Dick Diver – not to mention Fitzgerald's earlier heroes, Amory Blaine and Anthony Patch – are financially if not morally aided by others. Stahr seems provincial when compared to Gatsby and especially Dick Diver; but in his provinciality lies his special strength, he is narrow but profound, distinctly American in the high order of his specialized knowledge. Fitzgerald's other heroes are intricately involved with the very rich, and the consequences of their lives depend upon how they differ from them; Stahr never seems deeply concerned with wealth, he assumes it as part of the 'grandeur' that he 'demands of life'. He lives and works in the business world of Hollywood but he is not a businessman. As Boxley, the English script writer recognizes, he is first and last an artist. And it is this artistic self of Stahr, that creative aspect of his nature that identifies him with his creator and takes him to the state of being an asrchetypal hero whose tragic destiny embodies both the possibilities and the shortcomings of the legendary dream. He is 'the last of the princess' who dies for what he believes in.

The concept of heroism, especially in terms of its relationship to past American culture, is constantly before the reader. In the first chapter, Cecilia goes with Manny Schwartz, a defeated producer, and Wylie White, a cynical script writer, to the 'Hermitage, Home of Andrew Jackson'. It is dawn and Wylie comments, "I was born never here – the son of impoverished southern paupers. The family mansion is now an outhouse". (p.10) The sense of decay is emphasized more significantly when Wylie and Cecilia leave Schwartz, who will soon commit suicide, at Jackson's home and Cecilia observes:

> He had come a long way from some ghetto to present himself at that raw shrine. Manny Schwartz and Andrew Jackson – it was hard to say them in the same sentence. It was doubtful if he knew who Andrew Jackson was as he wandered around, but perhaps he figured that if people had preserved his house Andrew Jackson must have been someone who was large and merciful, able to understand. At both ends of life man needed nourishment: "a breast – a shrine". (p.13)

The contrast between an American past of rugged individualism and a present that is filled with destructive commercialism is of course dramatized by Stahr, who as the last hero seems already rather old-fashioned."He was a marker in industry like Edison and Lumiere and Griffith and Chaplin" – His achievements are in the past, he has no future. Fitzgerald does not permit us to forget the heritage that has been desecrated. In a later scene, after Stahr has told 'the money men' of Hollywood that they should sponsor a picture that will lose money because it is a 'quality picture , he walks into the commissary with his guest, Prince Agge of Denmark, who sees an actor dressed like Abraham Lincoln:

> . . . his kindly face fixed on a forty-cent dinner, including dessert, his shawl wrapped around him as if to protect himself from the erractic air-cooling – now Prince Agge, who was in America at last, stared as a tourist at the mummy of Lenin in the Kremlin. This, then, was Lincoln. Stahr had walked on far ahead of him, turned waiting for him – but still Agge stared. This then, he thought, was what they all meant to be. Lincoln suddenly raised a triangle of pie and jammed it in his mouth, and, a little frightened,

Prince Agge hurried to join Stahr.[19]

Finally, Fitzgerald makes the explicit connection between Stahr and Lincoln: "Stahr like Lincoln was a leader carrying on a long war on many fronts; almost single-handed he had moved pictures sharply forwards through a decade, to a point where the content of the 'A productions' was wider and richer than that of the stage. Stahr was an artist only, as Mr. Lincoln was a general, perforce and as a Layman". (p.106) It is clear by this point in the novel that Fitzgerald's central intention is to examine the loss of idealism in America, that Stahr is the last of such heroes as Jackson, Lincoln, Edison, Lumiere, Griffith, and Chaplin. "Don't start trusting Americans too implicitly", Stahr tells Kathleen, his English girl friend, "they may be out in the open, but they change very fast . . . very fast and all at once, . . . and nothing ever changes them back". And she responds: "You frighten me. I always had a great sense of security with Americans". (p.115) In the last chapter of this unfinished novel, Fitzgerald has the American individualist, Stahr, confront the Communist Brimmer. Stahr is at his weakest, defeated in love and soon to be defeated in his work, no longer the 'technological virtuoso' of his youth; when he grows helplessly drunk, Brimmer looks with contempt upon him and thinks: "Is this all? This frail half-sick person holding up the whole thing". (p.127)

Fitzgerald meant 'this frail half-sick person' holding up the old virtues – tolerance, kindness, forbearance, affection – against the mechanized world of modern America, Stahr's failure to maintain the traditional individualism depicts the tragedy of American idealism. In the summary of the plot, as Fitzgerald foresaw: "Stahr for the first time visits Washington with the intention of seeing the city; and it is to be presumed that the author had meant to return here to the motif introduced in the first chapter with the visit of the Hollywood people to the home of Andrew Jackson and their failure to gain admittance or even to see the place clearly: the relation of the moving-picture industry to the American ideals and tradition". (p. 129) Thus in his new novel Fitzgerald wished to dramatize the conflict between old idealism and the demands of the living reality – dramatize it in the portrait of Monroe Stahr, the idealist, enmeshed in the political and economic struggles of the day.

The Last Tycoon stands for Fitzgerald's 'unique achievement'– his ability "to establish that unmistakable moral attitude towards the world we live in and towards its temporary standards that is the basic essential of any powerful work of the imagination".[20] Though fragmented, it possesses all the essential aspects of a creative artist – intensity of feelings, effectiveness of imagination, maturity of vision, and great passion for work. In it Fitzgerald's literary motives and artistic skill being successfully combined present his 'wise and tragic sense of life'. Monroe Stahr's failure depicts the unfulfilled desires of his creator. As Bruccoli holds, Monroe Stahr is nothing but the "wish-fulfilment, and imaginative projection of Fitzgerald the unsuccessful screen writer who went to Hollywood in 1937 hoping to become a producer".[21] Stahr represents the gradual development of the romantic egotist introduced in Amory Blaine who for all his rebelliousness is in quest of values to build up 'the living consciousnes of the race' at the same time fulfilling his uniqueness. It is this quest of values in which Stahr finds his identity as 'the last tycoon'. With *The Last Tycoon*, Fitzgerald reaffirmed his link with the literary past. In Monroe Stahr's search of ideals and his identity Fitzgerald made his story "an escape into a lavish, romantic past that perhaps will not come again into our time".[22]

References

1. F.S. Fitzgerald, *The Crack-Up*, (ed. by Edmund Wilson), New York: New Directions Paperbook, 1956, p. 72.
2. Andrew Turnbull (ed.), *Letters of F. Scott Fitzgerald*, New York: Scribners, 1963, p. 269.
3. F.S. Fitzgerald, "Pasting It Together", *The Crack-Up*, p. 79.
4. *Ibid.*, p. 72.
5. *Ibid.*, p. 75.

6. Letters, p. 589.
7. F.S. Fitzgerald, "Early Success", *The Crack-Up*, p. 90.
8. F.S. Fitzgerald, "Notes", *The Last Tycoon* (ed. by Edmund Wilson), New York: Scribner's, p. 140.
9. F.S. Fitzgerald, "Notes", quoted from Sergio Perosa, *The Art of F. Scott Fitzgerald*, Ann Arbor: The University of Michigan Press, 1969, p. 163.
10. F.S. Fitzgerald, "The Note-Books", *The Crack-Up*, p. 109.
11. F.S. Fitzgerald, "Notes", *The Last Tycoon*, pp. 151-52.
12. F.S. Fitzgerald, "The Letters", *The Crack-Up*, p, 290
13. *Ibid.*
14. Mathew, J. Bruccoli, *The Last of the Novelists: F.S. Fitzgerald and The Last Tycoon*, London and Amsterdom: Southern Illinois University Press, 1977, p. 27.
15. F.S. Fitzgerald, "Notes", *The Last Tycoon*, p. 141.
16. Mathew, J. Bruccoli, *The Last of the Novelists*, p. 99.
17. William Troy, "Scott Fitzgerald – the Authority of Failure", Alfred Kazin (ed.), *F.S. Fitzgerald : The Man And His Work*, New York: Collier Books, 1966, p. 192.
18. Mathew, J. Bruccoli, *The Last of the Novelists*, p. 4.
19. F.S. Fitzgerald, *The Last Tycoon*, p. 49.
20. John Dos Passos, "A Note on Fitzgerald", Alfred Kazin (ed.), *F.S. Fitzgerald: The Man and His Work*, p. 156.
21. Mathew, J. Bruccoli, *The Last of the Novelists*, p.
22. F.S. Fitzgerald, "Notes", *The Last Tycoon*, p. 141.

The End of the Journey

AN artist is always a pilgrim in progress. The record of Fitzgerald's literary achievement confirms this idea. His was a journey from innocence to experience. From the 'romantic egotist' of the Jazzy twenties he grew up into the 'moral priest' of the depressing thirties. The 'golden boom' indulging in reckless gaiety and the 'dark period' experiencing crisis had somewhat parallel influences both on the personal life of F. Scott Fitzgerald and the national life of America. In fact, Fitzgerald utilized his own experience – a tragic experience on the whole – to represent the national experience and ultimately the human experience. He made the myth of success the basis for tragedy and transformed the self-made man into a tragic hero. He exposed the emptiness of contemporary social values and reaffirmed the moral values of the old order. Accordingly, the romantic attitude of the early fiction developed into the tragic vision of the mature works. The sentimental beliefs gave way to critical and creative intelligence.

All the heroes in Scott Fitzgerald's novels starting from Amory Blaine in *This Side of Paradise* to Monroe Stahr in *The Last Tycoon* in their search of different ideals represent man's quenchless desire to affirm, despite the voids and vicissitudes of the world, the perennial moral values of life. Almost as a rule, all of them start their journey as innocent – innocent not only in the sense of having pristine integrity of the naive, wild-eyed child-like selfhood, but also having an explicit faith in life and pre-conceived notions about the goodness of man. Experience comes to them through their confrontation with reality – both social and moral, which do not conform to their idealistic faith. They feel like refusing to accept the reality but cannot deny its being very much real. Since they are powerless to change the reality they live in, they brood, they suffer and get ruined at last. So Amory is left with crushed emotions; Anthony is damned with his 'very cravings for romance'; Gatsby dies with his loss of illusions; Dick Diver sacrifices his vitality and ambition; Monroe Stahr fails to hold the empire that he created. Their suffering disillusion them and give them an understanding of the world and life. In the process, they lose their innocence but gain in wisdom. Acquisition of knowledge and a sense of moral discipline help characters to acquire a new significance for remaining basically innocent even then. Here of course, I use the term 'innocence' with a wider connotation – innocence not as 'a product of nature' but 'the fruit of a disciplined life' springing from, 'order' and 'tradition'.[1] Fitzgerald, too, believed that 'innocence is no end in itself. . . . ' and the innocence he depicted is neither simply geographical or moral but is ákin to the eternal urge for perfection and immortality.

The novels of Fitzgerald with emphasis on innocent faith and destructive experience reveal the archetypal pattern of desire and disillusionment. Fitzgerald presented the traditional aspect of the dream through his idea of encounter between a vision of innocence and the reality of experience. In an ordinary and everyday dimension of life he depicted the age-old story of human aspirations and the sense of loss latent in it. To weave this parable of dream and disenchantment he chose primarily two themes of love and money. The love motif is always at the centre of his fiction and the experience of love is always brought to the foreground of action. Again this theme of love is mostly developed in close connection with the theme of money. Love stories are set in the social and cultural context of the leisure class or the 'very rich'. While establishing a close link between these two modes of experience he made his characters undergo a typical experience – entering into the world of alluring love and amazing wealth only to be ruined in the consequence, by betrayal of love and the carelessness or insesitivity of wealth. They are frustrated by the 'golden girl' and 'corrupt wealth'. The only exception is Monroe Stahr who as a result of his delay in taking decision loses Kathleen. Otherwise, the innocent hero has to bear invariably the loss of love, tyranny of wealth, waste of youth producing a sense of sheer futility and utter frustration.

Each of Fitzgerald's novels shows a change in the development and treatment of the material of his fiction. The varying interest for the theme bears a corresponding intensity of artistic realization of the material stating the gradual development of ideas and the maturity in thought and style of the artist. *This Side of Paradise* with its emphasis on cult of personality, the fabric of youthful and exuberant undergraduate days, sentimental attitude towards love and life, immature moral probings — suggest the author's intellectual naivety. *The Beautiful and Damned* reflects Fitzgerald's awareness of wider areas of American society where the young people get 'damned' with their desire to preserve youth and secure wealth. *The Great Gatsby* reveals the novelist judging rather than mere probing into the social values of a particular class that destroy the 'incorruptible dream' of Jay Gatsby. *Tender is the Night* conveys the author's mature impressions of the leisure class and his intuitive wisdom to warn against the moral chaos faced by Dick Diver. *The Last Tycoon*, even in its unfinished state, presents the persistent effort of Fitzgerald to write 'the novel of the age'. With this fiction the novelist reached 'the third act and epilogue' of his life. In writing this piece of work he felt a new lust for life and was able to regain his old ability and self-confidence to some extent. In a letter to this daughter the author wrote, "I am not a great man, but sometimes I think the impersonal and objective quality of my talent and the sacrifices of it, in pieces, to preserve its essential value has some sort of epic grandeur."[2] It is this 'impersonal and objective quality coming from his maturity of vision that gives a redeeming quality to his writings. Thus, Fitzgerald's artistry grew from the naive romanticism of *This Side of Paradise* to the more complex irony of

The Beautiful and Damned and gradually towards the more comprehensive form of tragedy in the later works. His passionate idealism was enriched by a tragic awareness of the paradoxes of life. He attained the power to create "an Apollonian vision of moral order and measured beauty".[3] The naturalness of feelings being combined with his deep insight and critical observation rendered a positive moral vision in a delicate poetic style. He matured in feelings. His ideas became more penetrating, observation more critical, perception more objective and craftsmanship more precise.

Fitzgerald, in the suffering of his heroes whatever may be the nature and degrees of distress, reflected the working of his everactive conscience in the midst of all turmoils. He transferred this awareness to his heroes so that their inner conflicts made their suffering more acute and painful. Either the protagonist himself or the narrator of the story like Nick Carraway in *The Great Gatsby* or Cecilia in *The Last Tycoon* observes the social and moral situation and offers a self-analysis. This self-awareness of Fitzgerald can be felt in varying degrees in different works by him. It is there in Amory's sense of despondency, in Anthony's discontented cry, in Gatsby's lament over the 'loss of illusions', in Dick Diver's disintegration and in Monroe Stahr's tragic fight to retain supreme power.

This strong sense of morality in Fitzgerald pervades all his writings. He wished to blend his creative intensity with the moral aliveness of the artist as a human being rather than with the sophistications of skill as a craftsman. I have, of course, emphasized mainly his novels as the author himself regarded novel to be "the strongest and supplest medium of conveying thought and emotion from one human being to another."[4] The study of his novels reveal that Fitzgerald, the dreamer, was a believer too. Despite his repeated failures he never gave up the beliefs he had been serving as the bedrock of his literary career. He maintained: "My generation of radicals and breakers-down never found anything to take place of the old virtues of work and courage and the old graces of courtesy and politeness."[5] Again and again he preached as well as practised his theory of 'great effort'. He wrote to his daughter about this noble conviction of his: "I never blame failure – there are too many complicated situations in life – but I am absolutely merciless toward lack of effort."[6] So when he dreamed of the limitless possibilities of life he trusted in man's ability and integrity. His dream of love and power was not without the faith in virtues of decency, honour and courage. And when he wished for the ordered social structures he believed in the role of individual in it. "I am interested in the individual," he wrote only in his relation to society. "We have wandered in imaginary loneliness through imaginary woods for a hundred year – Too long."[7] The principal characters in Fitzgerald's fiction always try to recreate the world around them. They wish to transform it through their noble aspirations not in isolation from, but in communion with society. Therefore, as Fitzgerald's career developed his choice of protagonists tended to shift from youthful dreams of 'inchoate rebelliousness' to active and creative ventures of Dick Diver and Monroe Stahr.

Moreover, Fitzgerald in his own self, combined the capacity of complete involvement and cool detachment. The innocent onlooker and the critical observer in him could envision the wide gulf between the dreamland of ideals and the material world of crude reality. So in the ecstasy of momentary happiness he could sense the inevitability of failure of the dreams. His double perspective could easily comprehend the inherent tragedy of the American experience. He had a fundamental sense of experience, and that fine instinctive sense made him a visionary – a seer.

For all the failure and futility that Fitzgerald found in the American experience his attitude was one of acceptance. He accepted the sadness of the tragedy of the world with a spirit of reconciliation. Fitzgerald's affirmation of faith in the promises of life and his conviction of man's struggle for ideal in the face of reality imparts an enduring quality to his works. He learned from his experiences that "life is essentially a cheat and its conditions are those of defeat, and that the redeeming things are not "happiness and pleasure' but the deeper satisfactions that come out of struggle".[8] Occasional cynicism of despair was submerged by "the wise and tragic sense of life". So to him, though at times America semed to be 'the story of the moon that never rose', yet in this very America only he could discover 'that quality of idea'—'the willingness of heart'. America to him was not simply a 'land' like France or mere 'people' like England. In watching 'the death struggle of old America' he envisaged tragedy of human experience. His characters in their pursuit of ideals embody man's generic need to thrust towards a self-realization – a consciousness that lies beyond the boundaries of any given time, space and reality. In recording the journey of the last of his dreamers – Monroe Stahr – from the poor boy to the 'last of the princes', he observed the "most beautiful history in the world. It is the history of me and of my people . . . . It is the history of all aspiration – not just the American dream but the human dream and if I came at the end of it that too is a place in the line of the pioneers".[9]

Fitzgerald's journey enacts the adventure of the early pioneers – the enchanted voyager setting out for the frontiers of experience. He was overwhelmed by the splendour and energy of American life. His 'capacity for wonder' and hope for the great promises – 'that something is going to happen' made him a lifelong adventurer. His affirmative and idealistic purposes and imaginative vision put him in the mainstream of the American writers for whom the beauties and impossibilities of the dream have been the chief motifs. He cherished the American dream as the root of a living culture and united it with the mainstream of tradition. Fitzgerald's great achievement to transcend the limits of vision and represent the human dream shows that the journey he had was not 'a meaningless extinction up an alley' but led to the broadways of human experience.

References

1. Cleanth Brooks, "The American 'Innocence' in James, Fitzgerald and Faulkner", *A Shaping Joy; Studies in the Writers Craft,* London: Methuen and Co. Ltd., 1971, pp.181-97.
2. F. Scott Fitzgerald, *The Crack-Up* (ed. by Edmund Wilson), New York: New Directions Paperbook, 1956, p. 291.
3. Robert Sklar, *F. Scott Fitzgerald: The Last Loncoon,* New York: Oxford University Press, 1967, p. 3.
4. F. Scott Fitzgerald, "Pasting It together", *The Crack-Up, op. cit.,* p. 78.
5. F. Scott Fitzgerald, *Letters,* ed. by Andrew Turnbull, New York: Scribners, 1963, p. 36.
6. *The Crack-Up,* p. 302.
7. F. Scott Fitzgerald, quoted from Robert Sklar's *The Last Laocoon,* p.302.
8. *The Crack-Up,* p. 306.
9. F.S Fitzgerald, "Notes" for *The Last Tycoon,* quoted from Mathew J. Bruccoli, *The Last of The Novelists: F. Scott Fitzgerald and The Last Tycoon,* London and Amsterdom: Southern Illinois University Press, 1977, p. VII.

Select Bibliography

Works by Fitzgerald

NOVELS

This Side of Paradise, New York : Scribner's, 1970.

The Beautiful and Damned, New York : Scribner's, 1960.

The Great Gatsby, New York : Scribner's, 1953.

Tender is the Night, New York : Scribner's,1951.

The Last Tycoon, New York : Scribner's, (ed. by Edmund Wilson), 1970.

SHORT STORIES

Flappers and Philosophers, New York : Scribner's, 1959.

Tales of the Jazz Age, New York : Scribner's, 1922.

All the Sad Young Men, New York : Scribner's, 1926.

Taps at Reveille, New York : Scribner's, 1935.

The Stories of F. Scott Fitzgerald, New York : Scribner's, 1969.

Afternoon of an Author, New York : Scribner's Paperback, 1968.

Six Tales of the Jazz Age, New York : Scribner's Paperback, 1960.

The Pat Hobby Stories, New York : Scribner's Paperback, 1974.

PLAYS

The Vegetable, or From President to Postman, New York : Scribner's, 1923.

MISCELLANEOUS

The Crack-Up, New York : Scribner's, (ed. by Edmund Wilson),1964.

The Letters of F. Scott Fitzgerald (ed. by Andrew Turnbull), New York : Scribner's, 1963.

Bits of Paradise, London: The Bodley Head, 1973.

Biography and Criticism

GENERAL

Adams J. T., *The Epic of America*, Boston:1931.

Aldridge, John W., *After the Lost Generation*, New York : McGraw Hill, 1951.

Beach, Joseph W., *American Fiction, 1920-1940*, New York : Macmillian, 1941.

---,*The Twentieth Century Novel, Studies in Technique*, New York: The Century, 1932.

Bewley, Marius, *The Eccentric Design*, London: Chatto and Windus, 1958.

Bishop, John P., *The Collected Essays*, New York: Scribner's, 1958.

Brooks, Cleanth, *A Shaping Joy; Studies in The Writers' Craft*, London: Methuen, 1971.

Cargill, Oscar, *Intellectual America: Ideas on the March*, New York: Macmillian , 1941.

Carpenter, F. I., *American Literature and the Dream*, New York: 1955.

Chase, Richard, *The American Novel and Its Tradition*, New York: Doubleday, 1958.

Cowley, Malcolm, *Exile's Return*, New York: The Viking Press, 1951.

Fiedler, Leslie A., *An End to Innocence*, Boston: The Beacon Press, 1956.

---, *Love and Death in the American Novel*, New York: Criterion, 1960.

Frohock, Wilbur M., *The Novel of Violence in America 1920-1950*, Dallas: The University Press, 1950.

Gardiner, Harold (ed.), *Fifty Years of the American Novel*, New York: Scribner's 1952.

Geismar, Maxwell, *The Last of the Provincials*, Boston : Houghton Mifflin, 1947.

Hassan, Ihab, *Radical Innocence*, New Jersey: 1971.

Hoffman, F.J., *The Modern Novel in America*, Chicago : Regnery, 1951.

---, *The Twenties: American Writings in the Postwar Decade*, New York: Collier Books, 1962.

Hutchens, J.K., *The American Twenties,* Philadelphia: Lippincott, 1952.

Kazin, Alfred, *On Native Grounds,* New York: Hitchcock, 1942.

Mizener, Arthur, *The Sense of Life in the Modern Novel,* Boston: Houghton Mifflin, 1964.

Perosa, Sergio, *The Art of F. Scott Fitzgerald,* Aun Arbor, The University of Michigan Press, 1969.

Shain, Charles, *F. Scott Fitzergald,* Minneapolis: University of Minnesota Pamphlets, No. 15, 1961.

Sklar, Robert, *F.S. Fitzgerald, The Last Laocoon:* New York: Oxford University Press, 1967.

Turnbull, Andrew, *Scott Fitzgerald,* New York: Charles Scribner's, 1963.

Trilling, Lionel, *The Liberal Imagination,* New York: The Viking Press, 1950.

Van Doren, Carl, *Contemporary American Novelists, 1900-1920,* New York: Macmillan, 1940.

West, Ray B., *The Short Story in America, 1900-1950,* Chicago: Regnery, 1952.

Wilson, Edmund, *A Literary Chronicle, 1920-1950,* New York: Doubleday, 1956.

Wright, Austin McGiffert, *The American Short Story in the Twenties,* Chicago: The University of Chicago Press, 1961.

SEPARATE ESSAYS

Adam, J.D., "F Scott Fitzgerald", *The American Mercury,* LXT, September 1945, pp. 373-77.

Barrett, William, "Fitzgerald and American", *Partisan Review,* XVIII, May-June 1961, pp. 345ff.

Berryman, John, "F. Scott Fitzgerald", *The Kenyon Review.* VII, Winter 1946, pp. 103-12.

Bezanson, Walter, "F.S. Fitzgerald. Bedevilled Prince Charming", *The Young Rebel in American Literature,* ed. by Carl Bode, New York: Preager, 1960, pp. 79-94.

Bewley, Marius, "F.S. Fitzgerald's Criticism of America", *The Sewanee Review,* LXII, Spring 1954, pp. 223-46.

Bicknel, J.W., "The Waste Land of F. Scott Fitzgerald", *The Virginia Quarterly Review,* XXX, Fall 1954, pp. 556-72.

Bishop John Peale, "The Missing All" in Edmund Wilson (ed.), *The Collected Eassays of John Peale Bishop,* New York: 1948, pp. 66 ff.

Buflin, E.C., "A Pattern of Parallel and Double. The Function of Myrtle in the Great Gatsby", *Modern Fiction Studies,* V. 15, 1969, pp. 517-24.

Burnham, Tom, "The Eyes of Dr. Eckleburg", *College English,* XIV, October 1952, pp. 7-12.

Cowley, Malcolm, "F.S. Fitzgerald. The Romance of Money", *The Western Review,* XVII, Summer 1953, pp. 245-55.

BOOKS AND COLLECTIONS OF ESSAYS

Bryer, Jackson R., *The Critical Reputation of F.S. Fitzgerald,* New Haven: Archon Books, 1967.

Eble, Kenneth, *F. Scott Fitzgerald,* New York: Twayne Publishers, 1963.

Goldhurst, William, *Fitzgerald and His Contemporaries,* New York: World Publishing Co., 1963.

Graham, Sheilah, *College of One,* New York: Twayne Publishers, 1963.

Hoffman, Frederick J. (ed.), *The Great Gatsby: A Study,* New York: Scribner's, 1962.

Kazin, Alfred, *F. Scott Fitzgerald: The Man and His Work,* New York: Collier Books, 1966.

Lehan, Richard, D., *Fitzgerald and The Craft of Fiction,* Carbondale: Southern Illinois Press, 1966.

Lockridge, Earnst, *Twentieth Century Interpretations of The Great Gatsby,* Englewood Cliffs, N.J.: Prentice-Hall Inc. 1968.

Miller, James E., Jr., *The Fictional Technique of Scott Fitzgerald,* The Hague: Martinus Nijhoff, 1957.

Mizener, Arthur, *The Far Side of Paradise,* Boston: Houghton Mifflin, 1951.

———, *A Collection of Critical Eassays,* Englewood Cliffs: N.J. Prentice-Hall, 1963.

Piper, Henry Dan, *F.S. Fitzgerald: A Critical Portrait,* New York: Holt, Rinehart and Winston, 1965.

Cowley, Malcolm, 'Of Clocks and Calendars", *New Republic,* VIV, March 17, 1941, pp. 376-77.

———, "Third Act and Epilogue", In Kazin, (ed.), *F. Scott Fitzgerald: The Man and His Work,* pp. 146-53.

———, "Fitzgerald. The Double Man", *Saturday Review,* XXXIV, Feb. 24, 1951, pp. 9, 10, 42, 43, and 44.

———, "FSF. The Romance of Money", *Western Review,* XVII, Summer 1953, pp. 246-55.

Doyno, Victor A., "Patterns In The Great Gatsby", *Modern Fiction Studies,* Vol. 12, 1966, pp. 415-26

Fiedler, Leslie, "Some Notes on F. Scott Fitzgerald", in *An End to Innocence,* Boston: 1955, pp. 174ff.

Fraser, John, "Dust and Dreams and the Great Gastby", *English Literary History,* V. 32, 1965, pp. 554-61.

Friedman, Norman, "Great Expectations and The Great Gatsby", *Accent,* XIV, Fall 1964, pp. 346-64.

Friedrich, Otto, "F.S. Fitzgerald. Money, Money", *The American Scholar.* XXIX, Summer 1960, pp. 392-406.

Frohock, W.M., "Morals, Manners and S. Fitzgerald", *The Southwest Review,* XI, Summer 1955, pp. 220-28.

Fussell, Edwin S., "Fitzgerald's Brave New World", *Journal of English Literary History,* XIX, December 1952, pp. 291-306.

Geismar, Maxwell, "F. Scott Fitzgerald. Orestes at the Ritz", in *The Last of The Provincial: The American Novel; 1915-26,* Boston: 1943, pp. 287 ff.

Giles, Barbara, "The Dream of S. Fitzgerald", *Mainstream,* X, March 1957, pp. 1-12.

Greenleaf, Richard, "The Social Thinking of Scott Fitzgerald", *Science and Society,* XVI, Spring 1952, pp. 97-114.

Hanzo, Thomas A., "The Theme and the Narrator of the Great Gatsby", *Modern Fiction Studies,* II, 3, Winter 1956-57, pp.183ff.

Harding, D.W., "Scott Fitzgerald", *Scrutiny,* XVIII, Winter 1951-52, pp. 166 ff.

Holmes, Charles S., "Fitzgerald: The American Theme", *Pacific Spectator* V.6, 1952, pp. 243-52.

Kuehl, John, "S. Fitzgerald. Romantic and Realist", *Texas Studies in Literature and Language,* I, Fall 1959, pp. 412-26.

Kuehl, John, "Scott Fitzgerald's critical opinions" *Modern Fiction Studies,* Vol. VII, No. 1, Spring, 1961, p. 4ff.

Lanter, Paul, "Plato's Stepchildren, Gatsby and Cohn", *Modern Fiction Studies*, V. 9, 1963, pp. 338-46.

Lucid, Robert F., "Three Public Performances: Fitzgerald, Hemingway, Mailer", *American Scholar*, V. 48, 1973-74, pp. 446-66.

Millgate, Michael, "Scott Fitzgerald as Social Novelist: Statement and Technique in the Last Tycoon", *English Studies*, XLIII, Feb. 1962, p. 1 ff.

Mizener, Arthur, "Fitzgerald and the Twenties", *The Paritsan Review*, XVII, January 1960, pp. 7-38.

———, "The Portable Fitzgerald", *The Kenyon Review*, VIII, September 1946, pp. 343-44.

———, "Scott Fitzgerald and the Imaginative Possession of American Life", *The Sewanee Review*, LIV, January-March 1966, pp. 66-86.

———, "Scott Fitzgerald. Moralist of the Jazz Age", *Harper's Bazaar*, N. 2863, September 1946, pp. 174-78.

———, "The Novel of Manners in America", *The Kenyon Review*, XII, Winter 1950, pp. 1-20.

———, "F.S. Fitzgerald's Tormented Paradise", *Life*, XXX, January 16, 1951, pp. 82-88, 91-98, 101.

Morris, Wright, "The Ability to Function. A Reappraisal of Fitzgerald and Hemingway", *New World Writing*, N. 13, New York: New American Library, 1958, pp. 34-51.

Ornstein, Robert, "Fitzgerald's Fable of East and West", *College English*, XVIII, December 1956, pp. 139-43.

Piper, Henry Dan, "The Lost Decade", *Interim*, II, September 1945, pp. 39-44.

Riddel, Joseph N., "F. Scott Fitzgerald, The Jamesian Inheritance, and the Morality of Fiction", *Modern Fiction Studies*, VII, 1966, pp. 331-60.

Shulman, Robert, "Myth Mr. Eliot, And The Comic 'Novel'", *Modern Fiction Studies*, V. 2, 1966, pp. 395-403.

Stallaman, R.W., "Gatsby and the Hole in Time", *Modern Election Studies*, 1, November 1955, pp. 2-16.

Taylor, Douglas, "The Great Gatsby Style and Myth", *The University of Kansas City Review*, XX, Fall 1952, pp. 30-40.

Trilling Lionel, "F.S. Fitzgerald" in his *The Liberal Imagination*. New York: 1980, pp. 243-54.

Troy, William, "F. Fitzgerald. The Authority of Failure", Reprinted in Kazin (ed.), *F. Scott Fitzgerald, The Man and His Work*. pp. 187-93.

Wescott, Glenway, "The Moral of Scott Fitzgerald", Kazin (ed.), *F. Scott Fitzgerald. The Man and His Work*, pp. 116-29.

Wilson, Robert N. "Fitzgerald as Icarus", *Anticoch Review*, XVII, Winter 1957-58, pp. 481-92.

Yates, Donald A., "The Road to 'Parádise': Fitzgerald's Literary Apprenticeship", *Modern Fiction Studies*, VII, Spring 1961, pp. 19-31.